GEORGE WHITEFIELD

George Whitefield

Preacher to Millions

By Mack M. Caldwell

THE WARNER PRESS

Anderson, Indiana

DEDICATED

to the

YOUTH OF THE KINGDOM OF GOD

with the

Hope

That They Will Be Helped

In Guiding Their Ambitions and Reaching

Their Ideals

by this

LIFE OF WHITEFIELD

INTRODUCTION

"It pleased God by the foolishness of preaching to save them that believe," said the apostle Paul.

Whitefield took that seriously and was willing to be called a fool, for Christ's sake. Men scoffed, but God blessed, and the great spirit of Whitefield still lives on in the hearts of those who love the souls of men. May our youth be fired with the evangelistic zeal and broad, unsectarian spirit of this "Preacher to Millions."

THE PUBLISHERS

CONTENTS

George Whitefield

CHAPTER I

BIRTH AND HERITAGE

One hundred and fourteen miles west of London, on a gentle slope overlooking the River Severn, lies the quaint old city of Gloucester. To the east it is sheltered by the Cotteswald Hills, and on the north and northwest by the Melverns and the hills of the Forest of Dean. There, with its antique gables and ancient cathedrals, this city stands out in one's mind as an historic city. In it the blood of martyrs was sacrificed for Christianity under the reign of "Bloody Mary." Near it William Tyndale, who gave the world a valuable English version of the New Testament, was born. It was in this city that the first Sunday-school was started by Robert Raikes, the originator of the Sunday-school idea. But Gloucester is of more interest to us at present, because it is the birthplace of the famous world evangelist, George Whitefield.

Thomas Whitefield, with his wife Elizabeth, lived in the Bell Inn at Gloucester and engaged in the business of selling wine and whisky. In this Inn, with its evil influences, a boy whom his parents named George was born on December 16, 1714. It is very doubtful if anyone dreamed at this time that this obscure babe would in a few years move the civilized world with his eloquence.

Only two short years after the birth of George his father died, leaving the care of seven small children with the mother. She was a woman with good judgment and a natural fondness for her children, especially her youngest. Something unexplainable caused her to expect more of him than she did of the other children. In order to provide food for the family Mrs. Whitefield continued her husband's business.

The children at the Bell Inn were subjected to the measles and owing to a lack of intelligent care the disease left George with a squint in one of his eyes. This remained with him throughout his life.

The general circumstances and environment of the Whitefield home were such as tended to evil rather than good. With his mother spending the time tending bar that should have been spent with George we are not surprized that he became wicked like those around him. In later life he described his mischievous childhood, telling how he would lie, cheat, and steal money from his mother's pocket while she slept.

However, his evil deeds were of that sort known as "pranks," and he never did go low into sin.

George's surroundings were made worse by the fact that in those days there was no public school system. There were here and there private schools, but only those who had considerable wealth could attend them. It seemed that George would never have the advantage of an education. And likely he never would have, had it not been for the fact that there was an endowed school at Gloucester in connection with St. Mary de Crypt Church. Here he started to school, but not until he was twelve years old.

During George's stay at this institution he developed an intense liking for reading and acting plays. He not only developed a liking in this direction; he became quite proficient as an actor, and showed considerable ability as an orator. When an assignment was given to him he gave much time to the preparation of his part, and soon there was a great demand for his services at exhibitions. His light hair and bright blue eyes made it easy for him to play the part of a girl—a part which he often played, and which filled him with shame afterwards.

The schooling at St. Mary de Crypt came to an abrupt close when at the age of fifteen George decided to return home and start to work with his mother at the Inn. He had come to that place in life that every boy must pass, where an immediate desire to be free from school discipline and go to work arrays itself in battle against the deeper desire to get an education and make a place for himself in the affairs of life. The desire to go to work got the better hold on him. He argued, "Too much learning would spoil me for a tradesman." Finally his mother agreed for him to quit all of his studies but one and begin work in the Inn. We shall let his own words describe what his work was like: "I put on my blue apron and my snuffers [to trim or extinguish the candles], washed mops, cleaned rooms, and, in one word, became professed and common drawer." We would express his thought today by saying that he was at times a janitor and at other times he was a bartender.

But even while he was doing this he would sit up late at night reading the Bible. Many were the nights and days in which he longed to be in school again. When anyone would speak of his going to Oxford his pathetic reply was, "I wish I could."

It is true that God works in mysterious ways. While Whitefield's environment was the worst his heritage was good. He desired to be a real man. There was no satisfaction for him in his present employment. The desire to become a preacher reached down to him from his great-grandfather. God visits good as well as evil upon children to the third and fourth generation. Even while the lad was tending the bar much of his spare time was spent composing and writing sermons. Once he unburdened his heart to his sister and said, "God intends something for me which we know not of."

Mrs. Whitefield's second husband, a Mr. Longden, influenced her to leave the Inn. When she went away the place was left in charge of one of George's elder brothers, whose wife was an enemy to George. This change in the business and home affairs only added fuel to the flames of discontent which soon burst forth, and resulted in a quarrel with the sister-in-law. For three weeks George would not speak to her, and being very uncomfortable and unwilling to do his part toward reconciliation he decided to visit one of his brothers in Bristol. Upon arriving in Bristol he was welcomed by the brother, who remarked, "Bristol is a splendid place for a holiday, and you may be able to find something to do here."

"I should like to be a clergyman; I really believe that I shall be one someday," answered George.

"Well, I must say that I do not see how your wishes are to be accomplished," replied the brother.

During this stay in Bristol, George found great delight in attending worship and in reading good

books. Especially did the *Imitation of Christ* fas-
cinate him. This book he read and pondered over
until he entered into an experience which he termed
"unspeakable rapture." In the midst of this religious
fervor he wrote to his mother and stated his determination never to return to his old employment as a
wineseller.

Two months was the length of George's visit in
Bristol and the length of his devotion and "rapture."
On returning home he fell into the company of wayward young men and these evil companions cor-
rupted his good morals. This, of course, was not
hard to do since he was idle. He was not in school,
he had no work and no purpose except that he would
not be a bartender. His fondness for reading plays
revived, and this was what he was doing when an
incident occurred that changed the whole course of
his life.

A young man who was working as a servant at
Pembroke College, Oxford, visited the Whitefields.
When he told them that he had earned more than
his expenses by work, Mrs. Whitefield said, "This
will do for my son." Then she turned to George and
asked if he would go. "With all my heart!" was
his ready answer. Plans were made immediately for
his preparation for college.

George returned to the school of St. Mary de

Crypt, where his studies were taken up with great determination. Again he yielded to various temptations, associated with some atheists, and soon accepted part of their teaching. But such a state did not long continue. While on an errand for his mother an impression came to him, stirred his feelings, and made him feel that he would become a preacher. When the impression was told to his mother she cried, "What does the boy mean?" and she commanded him to hold his tongue.

An elder brother who became disgusted with George's "alterations from saint to sinner and from sinner to saint," gave him a sharp rebuke that served to lessen his self-confidence and make him more watchful.

Chapter II

AWAY TO OXFORD

The often repeated and deeply rooted desire of George Whitefield to go to Oxford was realized in 1732, when he was about eighteen years of age. At that time, with a loan of nearly fifty dollars from one of his friends and the recommendation of several others, he entered Pembroke College, which was a part of the great University of Oxford, as a servitor. In this position he was partly supported by college funds and partly by waiting on tables, blacking boots, and knocking on the doors at bed-time to see if the students were in their rooms.

This work, tho considered low by most of the wealthy students, was a pleasurable promotion for the former mop-washer and wine-seller of Gloucester. Even tho many of the students were guilty of rioting and excesses they were socially and intellectually far above the scamps who drank at the old Bell Inn. Young Whitefield enjoyed his position greatly, for even tho his place was not altogether satisfactory, would we not expect him to do what thousands of other poor boys have done—sacrifice present pleasure for future profit? Being at the age when youth dreams and has great aspirations and

At Pembroke he waited on tables to help pay his expenses.

hopes for the future, this servitor looked on into the
golden years ahead when he might be a help to
humanity. He dreamed of the day when he might
be a servant of God in the office of a minister. Thus
hopefully and faithfully he went about in the daily
routine of his duties.

Having developed ability to read well and being
of a serious turn of mind, Whitefield seldom lost
an opportunity to read. As it had been at home, at
St. Mary de Crypt, and at Bristol, so it was at
Oxford—we find our young hero with a book.

Two books that Whitefield read at this time were
Law's *Serious Call to a Devout Life*, and a book
on *Christian Perfection*. He was fairly well con-
tented before reading these books, but soon after he
became greatly agitated in mind. Instead of comparative peace with regular attendance at services
of worship and commendable devotion to works of
charity, he began to feel that he was not yet safe.
He became conscious of the fact that his deeds, for
some cause or other, were not acceptable to Him
whose eyes behold both evil and good.

The spiritual atmosphere of Oxford and the country as a whole was not such as would benefit and
encourage the seeker of a devout and an exemplary
life. The Parliament had passed a law that all
preachers in the Church of England and all leaders

in English colleges should conform to the formal
regulations of the state church. Such a decree could
have nothing but a deadening effect on the spiritual
life of the nation. Serious-minded and spiritual men
at once withdrew from their churches and teaching
posts rather than accept a form of worship that
would hinder the power of God from working.

An educational system inducing none or very few
to seek after God is, indeed, in need of reformation.
And a religious system called a church in such a
condition is deplorable. But such conditions pre-
vailed while the Gloucester youth was at the famous
University.

The one ray of light to Whitefield was a group
of young men who had formed themselves into a
kind of society for the cultivation of the religious life.
They met often for prayer, edification, and Bible
study. Their manner of life was such as would
attract attention from all and ridicule from the
thoughtless and the ungodly. This band imposed
upon themselves most drastic regulations. Altho
it was done with good intentions they practised a
very unnatural outward piety. Strictness to the line
and to the letter was their idea of perfection. To
waste a moment of time was almost a hideous sin.
Doing works of social service, attending worship,
saying prayers, and taking communion were to them

the only proper way that a Christian should be employed. Besides the practises just mentioned much self-denial was practised. In this they often did acts of penance similar to those done by the monks of the Dark Ages. Living by a set rule or method was such a common practise among them that they were nick-named "Methodists." Another name by which they were called, in ridicule, was "The Holy Club."

As Whitefield observed the manner in which these young men returned good for evil he was convinced that what they had he needed. When they were mocked, scoffed at, shoved about, and had dirt thrown upon them they showed no desire for revenge. George desired to possess such a temper within himself. He longed to become one of the holy band, which numbered then about fifteen. Of that number John and Charles Wesley were the leaders.

While out on an errand of mercy Whitefield saw a woman who was about to commit suicide. He at once sent word to Charles Wesley to visit her. When the younger Wesley learned from whom the request had come he became interested in Whitefield. Shortly an invitation to breakfast was given by Wesley. This meeting was the beginning of a life-time friendship between the two. The visit was also Whitefield's first actual contact with the "Methodists," a joy that he had looked forward to for months.

At the termination of the visit Wesley loaned him two books. The title of one was *The Fear of Man*, and that of the other was *A Country Parson's Advice to His Parishioners*. These he read, and revived his "good works." Later another book was loaned him by the same friend. It was written by a Scotchman of great spiritual attainments whose name was Henry Scougal. The name of the book was *The Life of God in the Soul of Man*. The burden of its message was to show that salvation could not be obtained merely by charitable gifts and deeds, adhering to a form of religion, and leaving off common sins. And this was exactly the message that Whitefield needed. He had been seeking life—active, joyous, everlasting life, but he had erred in the manner of his search.

From the book he learned that salvation was by grace through faith in the Son of God. As he read "that true religion is the union of the soul with God, and Christ formed within us," the Holy Spirit illuminated his mind. Suddenly he realized that he must have a regeneration. But he was not yet where he could have the means of grace applied to his own soul.

As the Wesleys were recognized leaders in relig-

ious matters he looked to them for help. Charles
Wesley realized the state of mind of Whitefield and
sent him to John for counsel. The doctrine of the
new birth was almost unknown in the pulpits of the
land at that time. The real experience of the new
birth was unknown to most of the Methodists. While
they were teaching they were in great need of being
taught. John Wesley now made the mistake of trying to teach what he had not experienced, a mistake
that has been repeated a thousand times since his
day. The instruction given was all about externals,
or outward actions.

From this advice our truth-seeker was led to revive
the old legal system of salvation by works. With
crushing exactness he took the sacrament every Sunday. He fasted on Wednesdays and Fridays. He
denied himself of all fruits, which were exactly what
he needed, and gave precisely one hour a day to
works of charity! He had a program for life!

This program was too unnatural and rigid. It
hindered his studies. His determination was "to
study to be a saint rather than a scholar," and the
truth is that he was making no success at either.
Having come out openly with his profession he
began to receive a true Christian's persecution without a true Christian's experience and grace to bear
it. He was hissed at; he had dirt thrown upon him

by his enemies, and he was shunned by his friends. The headmaster threatened to expel him from school if he went to another meeting of the "Holy Club."

However bad these outward troubles seem, it was the inward troubles that were tormenting him. The shackles of methods were too heavy for him to bear. His constant and severe self-examination kept up a storm within his soul. He was one who was going from bad to worse, and the combination of troubles overcame him.

Concerning his state at this time he says, "My memory failed me. My whole soul was barren and dry. When I kneeled down I felt great heavings in my body, and I have often prayed under the weight of them till the sweat came through me. For some weeks I scarcely slept for three hours at a time.

"God only knows how many nights I have lain upon my bed groaning under the weight I felt. Whole days and weeks I have spent in lying prostrate on the ground. Self-love, self-will, pride, and envy buffeted me in their turns, but I was resolved to die or conquer.

"Having nobody to show me a better way, I thought to get peace and purity by outward austerities. I always chose the worst sort of food, tho my place furnished me with a variety."

In a certain book he chanced to read that one

must mortify the will to become godly. He thought that was good, for the Bible said to leave all. So he proceeded to mortify his will by doing unpleasant things and refusing to do that which he enjoyed. Even attendance at "Methodist" meetings was stopped. Long hours were spend in seclusion and on long walks into the fields alone.

Lent came on and served only to increase his trouble. In order to free himself from it he intensified his self-mortification and penance. Some days he did not eat at all. When he did eat he refused everything but sage tea without sugar in it and some coarse bread. It was during the last week in Lent that the break came. He collapsed physically and sent for his teacher. The teacher at once called a doctor. The sick youth was immediately put to bed and steps were taken to restore him to health.

Altho the sickness was a burden physically, it was a burden-bearer spiritually. There in the quiet of the sick-room the soul of the patient was earnestly seeking God. His seeking was abundantly rewarded one day when, suddenly, light came into his soul and revealed the way of salvation. The way was made so plain that he was able to grasp the promise by faith and accept deliverance. Then came overwhelming peace that continued until it was "joy unspeakable and full of glory."

After a time Whitefield was improving rapidly physically, and when he was able to be up and about a little the physician advised him to go home for rest. The "rest" period that followed is a very interesting and dramatic part of his life story. For one who had found such a joyful union with Christ idleness was well nigh impossible.

Almost as soon as he reached home he began what we now call personal evangelism. A lady who had enjoyed his reading of plays was visited. In a short time she was led into the kingdom of God and became the first member of the first Methodist society in Gloucester. This was not the only one who was visited. Friends one by one were led into the new life. These converts were formed into a regular society with regular meetings. In these meetings the coming evangelist prayed and read the Scriptures. Much effort was spent in the cultivation of his devotional life. The Bible was read daily. Much time was spent in praying over it and for the new converts. Thus Whitefield was led into new light, life, and power.

CHAPTER III

ORDINATION AND FIRST SERMON

Those who understand Whitefield's character and manner of life do not question the judgment of his friends in urging so young a man into ordination. He was pliable, we are told by Wesley, in regard to the things that concerned himself. But concerning the things of God he would not deviate an atom from either a principle or a matter of conscience. His convictions were clear and he stood staunchly for them.

He possessed tact and zeal that were commendable. He proved himself in college life. And since he had returned to his home town his life had been very exemplary. It was clear to all who cared to see that he was a proper candidate for the office of a bishop.

Other things that indicated his fitness for the pulpit were a rich mellow voice and a perfect naturalness and grace of movement which were exceptional.

Yet with all of these characteristics he was very meek and humble. His great humility, and it is safe to say considerable timidity, caused him to pray that he would not be ordained. He hoped that if he should be, that it would not be for some years yet.

He even asked his Oxford friends to pray against his being ordained, but they prayed for it instead of against it.

Once about this time he had a dream which was looked upon as having special significance. In the dream the bishop gave him some gold. As he received the coins in his hand they were heard to jingle. He believed this was a token of his ordination, and that soon he would be, as they expressed it then, "in holy orders." A little later when he was returning from the cathedral where he had been attending a prayer-meeting he was called by a messenger and told that the bishop wanted to see him. With fear and trembling, and no thought of ordination, he started to the bishop's palace. Accusations overtook him on the way and he wondered what he had done to deserve a rebuke from the bishop. The young man gave himself a thorough and not altogether pleasant self-examination. Then he rapped at the door of the palace.

As soon as the bishop had received and welcomed Whitefield he excused himself and went out to change his habit. The caller was glad for these spare moments alone and he used them for prayer. In a short time the bishop returned. In a very friendly manner he began to relate how that Whitefield had been recommended by his friends for ordination as a deacon. The bishop also stated that from personal observation he knew his character and liked his behavior in church. After learning that Whitefield was twenty-two years old he said, "I have declared I would not ordain anyone under three-and-twenty, yet I shall think it my duty to ordain you whenever you come for holy orders." The good bishop made him a present of five guineas ($25.55), which jingled in his hand, and the young minister went away very happy, indeed, because his dream was coming true.

June 20, 1736, was the day of his ordination as a deacon. On the preceding Saturday the candidate spent two hours outside the city in prayer. And as to what took place Sunday morning he says, "On Sunday morning I arose early and prayed over St. Paul's epistle to Timothy, and more particularly over the precept, 'Let no one despise thy youth.' When the bishop laid his hands on me I offered my whole spirit, soul, and body to the service of God's sanctuary; and afterwards sealed the good confession I had made before many witnesses, by partaking of the holy sacrament of our Lord's most blessed body and blood. I hope the good of souls will be my only principle of action."

Now, before he had time to think where or when he would preach his first sermon, his friends were requesting that he preach in the afternoon of the day of his ordination. This, however, he refused to do, partly because of the sacredness of the responsibility, but mostly because he had a foolish notion that he ought to have a hundred sermons written out before he was ready to preach one.

June 27, exactly one week after the ordination took place, he preached his first sermon. This first sermon was not out in some out-of-the-way place; neither was it in some small village, but right in the center of Gloucester, in the church of St. Mary de Crypt where he had attended worship as a child. The subject for the occasion was, "The Necessity and Benefit of Religious Society." There were in the audience relatives, including his mother, friends, curiosity seekers, scoffers, and some who were indifferent. The sight of an unusually large audience frightened him, but in the course of the sermon he mastered the situation and was enabled to speak with "gospel authority."

As to the results of the sermon it was a benefit to many. Someone who was an opposer reported that fifteen people had been driven mad by the sermon. When this report came to the bishop he expressed a desire that the madness would last at least to the next Sunday.

The new preacher was perhaps as dissatisfied with

his sermon as anyone. He sent it to an experienced clergyman as proof that he was unfit for the ministry. The clergyman thought it was excellent and divided it into two sermons for his own people. One of them he preached in the morning and one in the evening. After two weeks the sermon was returned with five dollars and eleven cents to pay for the use of it.

Two days after this first sermon was delivered Whitefield preached again and strongly condemned the sins of polite society. On the following day he returned to Oxford. In a week from the time he returned, he exchanged the clothes of a servitor for the gown worn by a bachelor of arts.

The Oxford Methodists soon made Whitefield their leader. For a while he had great enjoyment preaching for them, pursuing his studies, and visiting. One thing that was especially enjoyed by him was the study of Matthew Henry's Commentary, a set of books which he had bought on credit. The privilege of reading these books quietly was "sweet retirement" to him.

Chapter IV

EARLY POPULARITY

The time in which one lives has much to do with the shaping of his life. Reference has been made in a former chapter to the religious and social condition of England in Whitefield's day. A further description of these conditions is needful here in order for us to appreciate the career of the young preacher.

In regard to spiritual conditions it would not be enough to say that the situation was deplorable. To say that spirituality was at a low ebb would hardly do, for there was no spirituality, comparatively speaking. True enough there were some ten thousand clergymen being supported by the state. But what could they do to convert the nation when most of them had not been converted? They were busy preachers, but their time was not spent in preaching. Fox-hunting, racing, card-playing, and other things of like nature occupied much of their time. Reveling was the order of the day for all who chose to do such things, and the majority made such a choice.

The preaching of the day was without either the gospel or gospel authority. It was not preaching at all. It consisted of abstract and lifeless essays read from the pulpit in an uninteresting manner. The

famous jurist, Mr. Blackstone, visited all of the
leading churches of London. After his circuit of
observation was completed he made the statement
that there was no more Christianity in the pulpits
of London than there was in the writings of Cicero,
the pagan Roman!

One minister is known to have said, "A converted
minister was as great a wonder as a comet."

The social status of the land was still more shock-
ing. Immorality was painfully common. Many
marriage ceremonies were performed when both
parties were under the influence of whisky. Some
would be hardly conscious enough to know what was
going on. Then they would become sober and learn
that they had been married to someone who was
almost unknown to them. Personal purity was considered practically an impossibility. Vice was not
confined to the low classes. Some of the young men
of the royal families were taught "the art of seduc-
tion" as a necessary part of a thorough education.

Theaters at this time were exceptionally foul.
Women who insisted on seeing the plays would wear
veils or masks over their faces to hide their identity.
The popular books of the day were as vile as the
shows. Yet they occupied a prominent place in most
of the homes.

Drinking intoxicants was almost as common as

eating. Most people thought it was proper. The Prime Minister drank. Parliament held session while its members were under the influence of alcohol. Many preachers drank. Distillers and saloonkeepers were plentiful and realized a good business. It is said that every sixth house in London was a saloon. One tavern boldly displayed a sign: "Drunk for one penny, dead-drunk for twopence, clean straw for nothing!" When the straw-covered cellar could accommodate no more the pavement outside would be thick with senseless drunks.

Naturally a place so degraded as this abounded with crime. London was so unsafe that no one dared venture out at night unless compelled to do so. Hold-ups were common, both in cities and in the open country. Travel was indeed dangerous.

In such a country, and out of such an environment arose suddenly a pure and fearless prophet of the Lord. His fame spread like a prairie fire over the nation.

As the preacher at Tower Chapel was to be away from his parish for a while he called Whitefield to serve in his absence. The place was accepted and Whitefield preached his first sermon in London on August 8, 1736. Every succeeding sermon drew more people until the chapel would not accommodate all those who wanted to hear.

Always fresh, spirited, and seasoned with good judgment and love he never failed to impress his hearers. As much as the qualities mentioned, his industry gave him much publicity. His week's work in this supply pastorate was a sermon each Tuesday to the prisoners, a prayer-meeting morning and evening at another chapel, a daily visit to soldiers and patients in hospitals, and a sermon and catechetical class each week.

After serving the two months at Tower Chapel Whitefield went back to Oxford for a few weeks. But one place could not hold him long because his fame had gone abroad and he felt an inward urge to preach incessantly. Soon he was called to supply for a preacher in Hampshire. He answered the call and went. The low, uncultured class of people to whom he preached at Hampshire were a sore trial to his refined and sensitive disposition. Realizing that it was the common people who heard Jesus gladly, Whitefield determined to become reconciled to the situation. Soon he says he was enabled to enjoy their company and learn more from them than he could learn in the same length of time at the University.

His determination to work and make every moment count increased with his popularity. His schedule for the day now consisted of eight hours for study, eight hours for visiting and personal work, and eight hours for eating and sleeping. This plan for the day was a little more severe than the plan of Alexander the Great. He advised eight hours for sleep, eight hours for work, eight hours for recreation.

John Wesley, who had gone to America to do missionary work among the Creek Indians, wrote a letter to Whitefield explaining the need of workers, and Whitefield desired to go at once. This desire became more intense when Charles Wesley returned to England for the purpose of getting recruits. Whitefield would have sailed immediately, but there was a continued delay of the voyage. However, no time was lost waiting for the ship to sail. Whitefield plunged into an itinerary of evangelistic preaching that increased his sudden popularity. He had great success at Bristol, where a large congregation attended his meetings. Here he was heard by his brother who had said a few years before that he did not see how George would ever become a preacher. Calls came pouring in from every direction. He was invited to preach at Bath, the most fashionable resort in England. Fearlessly he denounced the sins of polite society, and still his congregations were large. Multitudes would be turned away for lack of seating room.

His labors during this period were a great delight to his soul. He described his joy in the following words: "I found uncommon manifestations granted me from above. Early in the morning, at noonday, evening, and midnight, nay all the day long, did the blessed Jesus visit and refresh my heart. Sometimes, as I have been walking, my soul would make such sallies that I thought it would go out of my body. At other times I would be so overpowered with a sense of God's infinite majesty that I would be constrained to throw myself prostrate on the ground and offer my soul as a blank in his hands, to write on it what he pleased."

We soon find him back in London preaching nine times a week in whatever church desired his ministry. He preached nine sermons a week, and the congregations grew larger. People flocked to his meetings. They pressed around him in the streets until he was unable to walk from place to place because of the crowds. It became necessary for him to ride in a coach wherever he desired to go.

The surprizing thing about the large attendance at his meetings was the fact that people came right on while he condemned their sinful practises and exposed their wickedness. This preacher had a distinctive message. In a time when most people had a profession without the new birth he proclaimed to all that they must be born again. He declared positively that without the new birth they could not be genuine Christians. Such a message was almost unheard of then. Wherever it was preached a reformation followed.

Whitefield, now twenty-two years old, had found his place in the work of God. As an evangelist he never feared that he would be without an audience, neither did he fear the audience after it assembled. He had plenty to say, had strength to say it vigorously, and enjoyed it with all his soul. However, there was one slight fear that came to him. Here he was, only twenty-two years of age, a graduate of a famous University, and without a rival as a popular preacher. Six years before this he was a common bartender! His fear was that such a sudden rise to popularity and fame would exalt him above measure. In order that such would not occur he prayed for humility, and his prayer was answered.

Chapter V

VOYAGE TO GEORGIA

A voyage across the Atlantic in the middle of the eighteenth century was neither pleasant nor safe. In fact it was extremely unpleasant and dangerous. Anyone who was traveling for pleasure would surely not "go abroad." Pressure or heroism, and sometimes both, were necessary to make one attempt an ocean voyage.

A view of conditions then will help us to see why this was true. Those were the days of sailboats, and therefore there was as much danger in a calm as there was in a storm. A continued calm meant that all on board would starve and be lost at sea. If there were a storm there was sure to be wind—the one supreme necessity for sailing vessels. Many are the tragedies that were caused by the calmness of the ocean. Ships would drift for days and days. Food would become less and less, and then give out, leaving all on board to die of starvation.

The sea-going vessels of Whitefield's time were small and inconvenient. Many of them had a single deck, were less than two hundred feet long, and had a small box-like place at each end for the passengers. From five to eleven weeks were required to sail from

Europe to America. The perils of sea travel then can be seen by comparing those ships with our present-day vessels. The trans-oceanic steamers that now cross the Atlantic in four or five days often carry as much as twenty thousand tons of cargo, and as many as fifteen hundred people. They are sometimes eight hundred feet long, and have every convenience found in a modern hotel.

Another thing that made ocean travel unpleasant in those days was the character of the sailors. The captain was usually cruel and tyrannical. The crews were composed of godless men who were anything but congenial companions.

Whitefield was not deterred from his purpose by any of these perils. They could not make him think of not going to Georgia, for to Georgia he was called.

The colony of Georgia was the farthest south and the youngest of the English colonies. It was chartered June 9, 1732. The following year James Oglethorpe landed with thirty-five families and settled at Savannah. Most of the first settlers were poor debtors who had been released from English prisons. Some were slum-dwellers from London and free convicts from British possessions. Later a better class came who were composed of Scotch Highlanders, English people, and Moravians. This col-

ony was governed by a board of twenty trustees,
with General Oglethorpe. Many of the trustees
were Presbyterians. Through their influence a law
was passed prohibiting the sale of whisky and the
ownership of slaves. In order to foster the religious
life of the settlers a chaplain was provided by law.

Adjacent to the colony there were some twenty-
five thousand Creek Indians with whom the settlers
traded. Oglethorpe did his best to be on friendly
terms with them. Trouble was caused, however, by
Mr. Bosworth, who was the first chaplain of the
colony. He proved untrue to his calling, married
an Indian, and raised an armed insurrection against
the settlers. The morality of the colony became
extremely bad. The conduct of some who professed
Christianity is manifest by the reply of an Indian
chief who was asked to become a Christian. He
said, "Why, these are Christians at Savannah!
These are Christians at Frederica! Christian much
drunk! ['Christian' had smuggled drink in.] Christian beat men! Christian tell lies! Devil Christian!
Me no Christian!"

To such a place as Georgia was, and to such a
mixture of people as lived there, Whitefield determined to carry the bread of life. Unaware of
Wesley's failure he was as eager to go to the new
world as Mr. Wesley was to return from it.

The Wesleys entered their new mission field with the wrong message. The "legalism," the stern methodical system of living by rule that they adopted for their own lives and urged upon the "Holy Club" at Oxford, was presented to the untrained, rude settlers, who were already filled with a burning hatred for tyranny. The result was that the preachers could hardly get an audience, and in addition to that discouragement they were hated, despised, shunned, and persecuted. The result of their work among the Indians was no better. In addition to the wars without, the worst war to John Wesley was that within his own soul. He said, "Thinking to convert the heathen Indians, I came to America; but oh! who shall convert me?"

Whitefield's decision to go to Georgia was firm, and he made the final decision without consulting either friends or relatives. They had discouraged his going before. Now he wrote to them and declared that if they would not promise to cease the opposition to his plans he would not visit them. They promised, and he paid a farewell visit to Gloucester. He was called upon to preach and great results followed his labors. As he left his home town the good Bishop Benson expressed approval of his determination to preach in America. He expressed faith in

Whitefield by telling him that he could do much good abroad.

About Christmas an opportunity for passage was offered to Whitefield on the *Whitaker*. This was one of a company of three transport vessels that were to sail soon, laden with soldiers. On December 28 he left London with thousands weeping, some looking on, and many seeking spiritual help. Two days later he went on board the *Whitaker*, expecting to sail at once. However, an unexpected delay postponed his sailing. They did not finally leave the English coast until February 2. During this interval he would preach daily "the unsearchable riches of Christ."

It was during this delay that his first sermons were printed. It happened that some charges were made against him by other clergymen. His friends insisted that his views be published in order to clear himself of the accusations. He had the sermons printed, partly to clear himself, but perhaps more than anything personal he wanted the world to know the Christ that he preached. At any rate, the latter seemed to be the most notable result. On both sides of the Atlantic his sermons were read by rich and poor, old and young. His published sermons were almost as fruitful in the salvation of souls as they were when delivered from the pulpit.

It happened that the ship which bore Whitefield put out from shore on the morning when the ship which brought Wesley from America landed. As soon as Wesley knew that his friend was sailing he cast lots for the purpose of seeing if Whitefield should sail. The lot drew the words, "Let him return to London." Wesley sent this to Whitefield and went on to London. Whitefield was "somewhat surprized," but went to prayer and was comforted by the passage in I Kings where we are told that the prophet of God, who was tempted to go back, contrary to God's express order, upon another prophet's telling him God would have it so, was slain by a lion.

As the *Whitaker* sailed down the English Channel many stops were made, and they were several weeks reaching Gibraltar. At first the young preacher-missionary was snubbed by the soldiers, who considered him out of his place. He bore it gracefully and was very careful of his conduct. Always he showed respect to the officers and when some of the soldiers were sick he was faithful to visit them. He would walk the deck in order to become friendly with the officers; he would visit the steerage for the purpose of adding the sailors to his list of friends. This practise was another instance of "becoming all things to all men" in order

to win them to Christ. The efforts he put forth in
this direction were not without results. Soon he was
a favorite with both soldiers and officers.

Having thus befriended himself with those on
board he had no difficulty in finding favor when he
landed. At Gibraltar, where they stopped for almost two weeks, he dined with the governor and had
many other courtesies shown him. The besetting sins
of this seaport town were those most often found in
such a place. They were drinking and swearing.
Whitefield had an opportunity to preach while
there. Drinking and swearing were the sins that he
condemned, and he did that with all the vehemence
of his soul. He visited the synagog of the Jews and
was graciously conducted to one of the chief seats.
He also visited the Roman Catholic church, but
nothing there was to his liking. When the ship was
ready to sail, over two hundred people accompanied
him to the shore. Many of them had been converted
or reformed by his preaching during his thirteen days
that he was there.

One day soon after they left Gibraltar a severe
storm arose. The waves dashed the little *Whitaker*
to and fro. The angry billows swept over the deck
of the reeling ship, and all of the passengers were
drenched time after time. Whitefield says, "I arose
and called upon God for myself and those that

He made friends with the sailors so that he might
win them to Christ.

sailed with me. . . . Then, creeping on my hands and
knees, I went between decks, and sang Psalms with,
and comforted the poor wet people. . . . I was enabled to finish a sermon before I went to bed, which
I had begun a few days before, and was never more
cheerful in my life."

Storms were not the only perils of this voyage.
An epidemic of fever broke out, and soon two of
the soldiers passed away. Others were sick, Whitefield among them, and he was brought very low.
Here is his pathetic record of his illness: "God has
been pleased to visit me with a violent fever, which
he, notwithstanding, so sweetened by divine consola-
tions that I was enabled to rejoice and sing in the
midst of it. Surely God is preparing me for something extraordinary, for he has now sent me such
extraordinary conflicts and comforts as I never before experienced. I was, as I thought, on the brink
of eternity. I had heaven within me; I thought of
nothing in this world; I earnestly desired to depart
and go to Christ; but God was pleased to order it
otherwise, and I resigned, tho I can scarce be reconciled to come back again into this vale of misery."

The *Whitaker* had on board one hundred people
in addition to the crew. Some entire families were
on board; so a number of children were present.
Whitefield always required obedience of them.

Once when a little fellow who was only four years old refused to say the Lord's Prayer, Whitefield gave him "several blows." The child at once complied with the instructor's wishes, and was given some figs as reward. At one of the prayer services an older child acted in a way that was unbecoming. Whitefield, who was chaplain, had him bound with ropes and would not let him go until he learned and recited the whole of the fifty-first Psalm to all who were on board!

During the whole of the voyage there were religious services. The captain of the sailors and the captain of the soldiers encouraged these services and enjoyed them. Whitefield would stand up to preach with a captain on each side, and men, women, and children gathered around. As has already been stated, two other ships sailed with the *Whitaker*. When the sea was quiet all three ships would come close together for a sermon. The preacher's excellent voice could be heard by all those on all three ships. Whitefield always preached the gospel with results, because he condemned sin and exposed that which was practised by those to whom he was speaking. On one occasion when he was preaching to the occupants of the trio of ships he had for a subject "The Eternity of Hell Torments." At the close of the service Captain Mackay asked the soldiers to

remain. When they did so he told them how he had
been addicted to the sin of swearing, but the influence of Whitefield's preaching had caused him to
"leave off" swearing altogether. He forcefully
urged them to do the same.

Thus a trip that is usually characterized by much
drinking, gambling, and swearing, was turned into a
veritable revival-meeting. Now no swearing could
be heard. Many had become Christians in the real
sense of the term. The young preacher had con-
quered the sea as he had the land.

A group of "pious souls" met the fleet which
landed at Savannah on the seventh of May, 1738.

Chapter VI

TURMOIL AND TEMPEST

Wesley's failure in Georgia seemingly would have discouraged Whitefield, but it did not. He would not talk of it and wrote nothing about it in his journal, but went to work with all his might to convert and teach the people.

The second day that he was in the colony he conducted services for those who came to him. His whole audience consisted of eighteen adults and twenty-five children. For the next few days he remained quietly in his room. This was done partly to avoid a collapse physically, since he had not completely recovered from fever, and partly because he was meditating on some plans for the future of the work.

However, his remaining quiet a few days did not avert a breakdown. It was on his second Sunday in America that his strength gave way and he could not preach a second sermon.

Soon he was back in the work again, visiting in various villages. On these visits he helped the poor, blessed the children, prayed for the sick, sang hymns to the discouraged, relieved the oppressed, and did all that he could in every way to lighten the burdens of the people and lead them to God.

These pastoral visits carried him among several races, and into all kinds of conditions. He met the rich, the poor, criminals, Indians, homeless, and orphans. Regardless of creed, color, or nationality, they all welcomed him, and he was pleased to do them good. The condition of the children was an ever increasing burden on his heart. A survey of the situation convinced him that the older people with their various beliefs and hereditary influences would be hard to form into a Christian church or community. He saw his one opportunity in the children. With them he determined to spend the greater part of his efforts.

Almost fifteen hundred dollars Whitefield collected and brought over from England for the purpose of building an orphanage. More funds were necessary, however, before anything of value could be started. But there must be something done at once. So Whitefield set about to establish schools of a religious nature in the villages. These were to help the children temporarily. He was aware of the fact that the hope of the church is always in the children. He saw also that they were in a helpless condition. Many of the orphans were quartered here and there in different homes with little or no care. Others were hired out and compelled to work long hours in the woods and fields.

Four months after his arrival at Savannah, White-field returned to England for the purpose of, being ordained a clergyman of the Established church. On August 27 he preached the farewell sermon, assuring the congregation that he would come back to them as soon as possible.

The return voyage to England was one of the roughest of all during his entire life of travelling. Like his stay in the new parish, the voyage was a kind of an endurance test. And a rather severe test it was. When the vessel had been out to sea about four weeks a gale arose from the east, and in a short while it was the cause of no little excitement. It became stormy and grew more and more fierce. Not only were the passengers excited but the sailors "reached their wit's end" and the captain was dismayed.

The vessel was tossed and thrown almost on its ends until much of the food and supplies were washed away. A goodly portion of that which remained was ruined. After they had been out five weeks, the allowance of water for each person was limited to one quart a day. The food consisted of salt beef and water-dumplings. A week later the daily allowance for each individual was reduced to a pint of water, two ounces of beef, and a small flour cake. What served further to discomfort the people was the fact that the weather grew worse and they knew not where they were! If ever they needed God it was then, and we are sure that there was one on board who was living close enough to God to reach him through prayer.

Soon land was seen and Whitefield exclaimed, "Blessed be the Lord God of Israel who, this day, hath visited a distressed people!" They landed on November 12 on the west coast of Ireland, at the mouth of the River Shannon.

If, like Paul, Whitefield was in perils very often, he was also like Paul in that he had correspondingly more abundant joys and rewards. In two of the largest cities of Ireland he met vast audiences, entered London amid applause, and found both the Wesleys converted and overjoyed to see him. He was courteously received by the Bishop of Canterbury and the Bishop of London, but more joyful to him than all of these was the presence of God while he preached or met with the societies.

On the day before Christmas he preached twice, "expounded" to two societies, and remained in prayer-meeting until after three o'clock on Christmas morning. On Christmas morning at four o'clock he preached, then again at six, administered the sacrament, preached three more sermons, and was in prayer till a late hour of the night!

A few nights later he spent practically a whole night in prayer with several other preachers. At the close of this devotion it was the conviction of all present that God would soon "do great things."

The ordination which brought him back to England was received on the fourteenth day of January, 1739. This final ordination brought much joy to his friends and was a blessing to the preacher himself.

Chapter VII

OPEN-AIR PREACHING

In the period which we have called Whitefield's early popularity we find openings almost everywhere for him. He was welcomed here and there, and he experienced little opposition. Now he entered into a period of intense persecution. Hated by the clergy, hissed at by the mob, he began to find some difficulty in securing a pulpit. The clergymen, many of whom were unconcerned about the new birth, and many more who thought that the application of water in baptism was enough, were now openly hostile to his work. Direct preaching on regeneration by Whitefield had made their position unsafe.

The natural result was that they began to deny him the use of their churches. Five refused him in one day. The idea that prompted the denial was that the young "enthusiast" would find himself without a church and be compelled to refrain from preaching.

Soon every church in London was closed against him. He must preach without a church or quit preaching, and quit he would not. In this circumstance the idea of open-air preaching occurred to him. But on consultation with his friends he was assured that such a method was a "bad notion" and that it would never be advisable to try it. However, the time soon came when the plan was to be tested out.

Whitefield said that since the churches were all closed against him and since they could not hold half the people who came to hear him, he would venture to preach without a church. At Bristol a minister refused the use of the pulpit and when asked why, he said, "Go to the chancellor." The chancellor also refused. Whitefield was now a preacher without a pulpit, but he had a burning message and a dauntless spirit that could not be stopped. On February 17, 1739, he stood on a small mound in an open field near Bristol. After a hymn was sung he began preaching on Matt. 5:1-3. Only about two hundred came. The next trouble appeared in the form of a summons to report before the chancellor, and Whitefield went immediately.

"Why are you preaching in Bristol without a license?" stormed the chancellor. Then without waiting for an answer he read from the canon to show that Whitefield's actions were illegal. "There is also a canon forbidding all clergymen to frequent taverns and play at cards. Why is that not put in execution?" asked the preacher.

"Why does not someone complain, and then they

would," was the reply of the chancellor. Then after threatening Whitefield with suspension and even excommunication, he let him go.

The following day Whitefield went to Kingswood, a mining district near Bristol. In a short time two thousand people had gathered for a sermon, and he stood up to preach. At this, his second outdoor service, the audience had increased from two hundred to two thousand. To this company he preached for an hour on John 3:3. It had come to pass that things designed by evil men to hinder the gospel were helping it. If the preachers had not opposed the evangelist thousands would never have had the opportunity to hear him.

The Kingswood coal-miners were, as a class, vile and filthy. They were a people who had been neglected and given up as hopeless. Yet they were hungry for the gospel. At the third service the crowd numbered four thousand instead of two thousand. And before long twenty thousand gathered to hear the gospel, some on foot, some on horseback, and others in carriages.

The preacher, who about a year before found it unpleasant to associate with illiterate people, was now almost overcome with joy at seeing scores of colliers turning to Christ at Kingswood. He says, "They were glad to hear of Jesus, who was a friend to publicans, and came not to call the righteous, but sinners to repentance. Hundreds and hundreds of them were soon brought under deep conviction, which happily ended in a sound and thorough conversion."

As he preached time after time, weeping in almost every sermon, multitudes who had never heard the gospel before were won to Christ. Concerning his tears, Whitefield would say, "You blame me for weeping, but how can I help it, when you will not weep for yourselves, tho your immortal souls are upon the verge of destruction, and, for ought you know, you are hearing your last sermon, and may never more have an opportunity to have Christ offered to you?"

About this time a revival was taking place in Wales and Whitefield made a journey there. He was greatly pleased with the leaders of the movement, Griffith Jones and Howel Harris. Harris disliked Oxford and was refused for ordination by the bishop, but he had been instrumental in reviving his home county and several adjoining ones. Jones was noted for his preaching to large gatherings at worldly celebrations.

One amusing incident of this trip happened at Cardiff. When the churches could not be had for services the town hall was secured. And while

Whitefield was preaching a bunch of mischievous boys tried to break up the meeting. They dragged a dead fox around outside the hall and chased it with a pack of hounds. It was difficult for the preacher to make the people hear about the disturbing noise, but with the power of his strong voice he was able to continue speaking.

Into many of the cities and villages of England Whitefield went and preached in churches, in halls, on hill tops, on vacant lots, and in fields. He was of the opinion that "There is something in this foolishness of preaching, which, when attended with a divine energy, will make the most stubborn heart bend or break." Here was a preacher whose natural talent was accompanied by divine energy, and he found his greatest enjoyment in the open fields. The pulpits being denied him, he had one made and moved it from place to place. Thus in his own portable pulpit, the green grass for a floor, and "the blue heavens for a sounding board," he said, "Field preaching is my plan. In this I am carried as on eagles' wings."

Chapter VIII

AT FAIRS AND RACES

Tho Whitefield was fond of preaching the gospel in the open fields he did not refuse an opportunity to preach in the churches. At times he would have been more pleased to preach in them. The pastor of the state church at Irlington invited the evangelist into his pulpit, and as prayer was being offered the church warden came in and made a disturbance. He demanded the evangelist to show his license. In order to keep down confusion Whitefield did not preach in the church. But in order to deliver his message to the people he preached in the churchyard later in the day.

As he could not use the church he determined to go to Moorsfield. When he expressed this determination the news spread so rapidly that before long it was the topic of conversation far and near. Some approved, some disapproved, while others felt a strange anxiety for the preacher. Moorsfield had once been a swamp, then a fashion parade, and now it was a sporting ground for all kinds of rude and sensual fellows. For a minister to go to this place to preach was, indeed, something that never had happened before.

Sunday, April 29, was the day appointed. And while the crowd was waiting for the preacher they amused themselves by laughing while some ruffians destroyed the table that the preacher was to use for a place to stand. Being of that class of men who find a way or make one, Whitefield found his way to a high wall that separated a part of the field from the rest. He climbed upon the wall and raised his hand for silence. As soon as he could be heard he quoted for a text, "Watch, therefore, for ye know neither the day nor the hour wherein the Son of man cometh." Now that the thousands were attentive he reasoned with them from the parable of the Ten Virgins. While he was speaking the scoffer, the mocker, the disturber, and the sportsman were all struck with awe. Those who came for violence stood mute and heard the words of the preacher. This sermon in such a center of devilish amusement gave those who were called the "Devil's castaways" a chance to hear the gospel.

On the same Sunday, late in the evening, Whitefield ventured into Kennington Common, the execution grounds, and preached there. It is said that from where he stood one could see the bodies of dead criminals hanging on the scaffolds. This, however, did not hinder the people from coming; for in a little while twenty thousand were gathered together. Many of them were soundly converted, and many more came with a gift for the orphanage at Savannah. The building of the orphanage was now the constant thought of Mr. Whitefield. The people were so moved by his appeal that in nine days nine hundred and seventy-two dollars were collected.

On Sundays the multitudes came to hear the word at Moorsfield, and on week days a similar crowd gathered on the Common. Whitefield continued to preach to them their duty and to gather funds for the orphanage.

It is reported that the singing of the congregation at the Common could be heard for two miles and that the voice of the minister could be heard one mile. Concerning the services at these places Whitefield said, "If this is to be vile, Lord grant that I may be more vile. I know this foolishness of preaching is made instrumental to the conversion and edification of numbers."

One day a letter came to Whitefield from Joseph Periam, who was an inmate of the Bethlehem Hospital. He had been placed there by his father and sister, who said that he was mad and should remain there until he had regained the use of his senses. The sister gave as proof of his lunacy that he had fasted for two weeks, that he would pray so vehemently that he could be heard four stories high, and that he had sold his clothes and given the money to the poor.

No doubt his "madness" is something that the world needs.

At the hospital he refused medicine because he was not sick. When he would not take the medicine five of the workers at the hospital threw him on a bed, pried his mouth open with a large key, cursed him, and gave him an oversized dose. The only explanation for their conduct was, "You are one of Whitefield's gang." At that time the man had never seen Whitefield.

At Northampton the fair-ground furnished a place for the hearers, and the race-track was used for a pulpit. Sometimes Whitefield stood at the starting post and pleaded for them to start for a better life. Once he preached on the steps of a wind-mill while three thousand people listened attentively.

It is needless to say that at this time he possessed a passion for souls. He not only did field preaching himself, but he was an encouragement to others to do it. His journal records a prayer that others would follow his example, "Lord do thou spirit up more of my dear friends and fellow laborers to go out into the highways and hedges, and compel poor sinners to come in."

One with such a burning for evangelical preaching could not help being disgusted with the prevalent powerless ministry. They called preaching on the new birth enthusiasm. To those who did this and thought that the Holy Ghost was not received now, he said, "Out of your own mouths I will condemn you, you blind guides. Did you not at the time of ordination tell the bishop that you were inwardly moved by the Holy Ghost to take upon you the administration of the church? Surely at that time you acted the crime of Ananias and Sapphira over again."

Whitefield never missed an opportunity to preach. When tired in body and even while sick and suffering pain, he went forth to the congregation. In clouds, in fog, in rain, and in sunshine he was faithful, and the sight of a crowd of hungry souls spurred him on when hindered by physical weakness.

On one occasion when upwards of fourteen thousand people were assembled he introduced Mr. Wesley. The flesh, says Mr. Wesley, was shrinking from the task, but a love for souls outweighed his love for "order" and he preached with good effect. At a late hour that night Whitefield "went to bed, rejoicing that another fresh inroad was made into Satan's territories by Mr. Wesley's following me in field preaching in London as well as in Bristol.

Lord, speak the word, and great shall the company
of such preachers be!"

People of opposing views and some of a trouble-
some disposition had done their part to oppose the
work of Whitefield. There had been some opposition from the beginning, but now the enemies of the
work found a new method of opposition. They
would circulate a report that Whitefield had been
mobbed or that he had died suddenly. In one place
nine thousand people were kept at home because of
such a report. He would be surprized to see people
run to him and rejoice that he was not dead.

At Tewkesbury the opposition seemed to be
united. The bailiffs did not want him to come.
When he did come four constables called to see him
and prevent his public preaching. These officers
came without legal authority. An attorney who was
friendly toward Whitefield demanded them to show
their warrant and they could not do so. They left
immediately and remarked as they departed that
the judge had determined to sentence Whitefield for
vagrancy if he preached there. In reply to this statement Whitefield quickly said, "No magistrate has
power to stop my preaching even in the streets if I
think proper." He did not preach in the town,
however.

These officers were told by Whitefield that their

public duty was to hinder evil doers and not ministers of true religion who were doing good. He further admonished them to be as particular about preserving order and peace at the horse races, balls, and festivals as they had been at the coming of the preacher.

Continuing his itinerary from town to town the preacher was threatened and forbidden, but he preached just as if the opposers had said nothing. Even Bishop Benson came in with the admonition that preachers should preach only where they had been authorized to preach by the bishop. Always alert with a reply, Whitefield said, "As for declining the work in which I am engaged, my blood runs chill at the very thought of it. I am as much convinced that it is my duty to act as I do, as that the sun shines at noonday. If you and the rest of the bishops cast us out, our great and common Master will take us up."

It now became difficult for Whitefield to find lodging in the Inns because of the excitement that was abroad. At one place in Basingstroke he was expelled from the room after he had gone to bed. Other places refused him. When he did find a place to lay his weary head a crowd of ruffians made sport of the place by turning loose a volley of fire rockets at the door.

The following day was a festival at the Basing-stroke fair-grounds. Showmen of various kinds, wrestlers, boxers, and a mixed multitude called the "rabble," were gathered together early in the day for sport and fun-making. Mr. Whitefield saw here an opportunity to speak for his "common Master" and at eight o'clock he preached to them. Many of them listened and there was no disturbance. After this sermon he started to ride away, but when he saw a new stage for the ungodly performers he determined "to bear witness against such lying vanities, let the consequences as to my own private person be what they would be."

He alighted from his horse, mounted the stage and "began to show them the error of their ways." A few appeared to be willing to hear the message, but every time the preacher attempted to speak his voice would be drowned by the yells and hurrahs of the rabble. Before he left the stage he was struck with a club, and as he left he was pushed and shoved until he could hardly get away. Concerning his feelings regarding the incident and the treatment he received, he says, "I got on my horse with unspeakable satisfaction within myself that I had now begun to attack the devil in his own strongholds and had born my testimony against the detestable diversions of this generation."

At the same place a band of ungodly fellows waylaid him with the intention of treating him so cruelly that he would not disturb their pleasure again. It so happened that he did not go where they expected him, and he doubtless escaped death at their hands.

At a place of revelry called Hackney Marsh he preached near the race-track while the horse races were going on. His reception here was not very kindly, but it was much better than that at some other places. Ten thousand people listened to him preach rather than to watch the races.

It has been declared that they which live godly in Christ Jesus shall suffer persecution, and it would be expected that one who lived godly and condemned ungodliness in such a generation would be severely persecuted. Whitefield bravely and patiently endured it all for the sake of Jesus, saying, "I am ashamed that I can do no more for him, seeing that he has done so much for me. His service is perfect freedom; his yoke is easy; his burden is light."

CHAPTER IX

"A TOUR ROUND AMERICA"

As an aid to an appreciation of Whitefield's experiences in travelling over America it is well for one to recall the America of that day. Vast changes have been made since the middle of the eighteenth century. The country then contained no city with a population of over twenty-two thousand. On Whitefield's first visit to Philadelphia the "City of Brotherly Love" contained probably twenty thousand people. A rapid growth during the next quarter of a century brought the population to thirty-two thousand. Philadelphia then prided herself as being the largest city in America. New York came second with a population of twenty-three thousand, while Boston ranked third with only sixteen thousand.

Travelling on land in those days was almost as unpleasant as travelling in the crude ocean vessels. This nation was "in the making," and had not reached the place where extensive road-building was considered practical. There were no roads then except in the towns and between some of the largest cities. There were no roads between the cities unless the cities were close together. Carriages were used in towns and cities, but a trip of any distance had to be made on horseback. On even a short journey one might have to travel over a trail through the forest, through dangerous swamps, and across streams without bridges. A long trip such as many of Whitefield's were, required wandering through forests where civilized men had not yet gone. Waterways were much used because of their comparative safety.

Whitefield never lived to see the popularity of the stage coach as a means of travel. The first one from Boston to New York was started two years after his death. The trip was made twice a month, and thirteen days of travel were required to make the distance.

No wonder that the roving Whitefield reached a town pale and exhausted! Riding all day and to a late hour into the night, sleeping in a poorly furnished cold room, arising for another day's travel, and repeating this daily for nearly two weeks would bring down more able-bodied men to weakness.

When Whitefield sailed for America in the summer of 1739, his mind was deeply concerned about his future work. While meditating on it he wrote, "I intend resigning the parsonage at Savannah." The small parish could not long contain a world prophet. He reasoned that if he resigned as chaplain at Savannah he could still care for the orphans and

also be "at liberty to take a tour round America."
In regard to such a course he further said, "I deter-
mine nothing: I wait on the Lord." He landed near
Cape Henlopen on the Delaware Coast and rode the
distance to Philadelphia—one hundred and fifty
miles—on horseback.

The preacher's fame had reached Philadelphia
before the preacher did and the inhabitants, one-
third of whom were Quakers, were glad to see him
and eager to hear him preach. Among those with
whom he made lasting friendships on this visit was
Benjamin Franklin, editor of the *Pennsylvania Gazette*, which was a popular paper. Franklin was one
of the most prominent printers in the country.

The church wardens and pastors showed him
much courtesy, and on Sunday he was invited to
preach. In order to show the desire some had to
hear him it is related that a Mr. Tennent, who
taught a Bible school, came twenty miles to see and
hear him. Like Mr. Franklin, Mr. Tennent became
a warm friend of the preacher's. One week was
spent in Philadelphia. It was a week of delight to
the visitor, who was given a hearty welcome and
had large congregations at his meetings.

Franklin attended Whitefield's preaching regu-
larly and was touched by the appeals for the support
of Bethesda, the orphanage at Savannah. However,

the famous printer wanted the orphanage moved to Philadelphia. When Whitefield could not be persuaded to move it there Franklin resolved to give nothing toward its support. His resolution was not carried out for the following reason as explained by Franklin himself: "I had in my pocket a handful of copper money, three or four silver dollars, and five pistoles in gold. As he proceeded I began to soften, and concluded to give the copper. Another stroke of his oratory determined me to give the silver; and he finished so admirably that I emptied my pocket wholly into the collection dish, gold and all!"

Another incident which happened at the same service shows the power of Mr. Whitefield to move men. One person who also wanted the orphanage moved to Philadelphia was so determined to give nothing that he emptied his pockets before leaving home. In relating the story Franklin says, "Towards the conclusion of the discourse, however, he felt a strong inclination to give, and applied to a neighbor who stood near him to lend him money for the purpose. The request was fortunately made to, perhaps, the only man in the company who had the firmness not to be affected by the preacher. His answer was, 'At any other time, friend Hopkinson, I would lend thee freely but not now, for thee seems to be out of thy right senses.' "

At these Philadelphia meetings many came to hear, and they were liberal in gifts of cash for the orphanage. Another result of his preaching, as one expressed it, was that it "threw a horrid gloom over the town" and "put a stop to the dancing schools, and every pleasant thing." This amusing remark shows that Whitefield never failed to condemn worldly frivolities.

Two invitations to visit New York had come to the evangelist. From Philadelphia he started on horseback, with Gilbert Tennent, a Presbyterian minister, and several others who were zealous for God. The little company edified each other as they rode along by each telling of his experience and the goodness of God to him.

On arriving in New York they were welcomed by Mr. Noble, who had given the invitation, but they were not welcomed into the churches. Both the English Church and the city hall were refused. Finally they found an opening at the Presbyterian Church. The house was filled night after night, and some could not find room to enter.

From New York back to Philadelphia was a preaching campaign with Gilbert Tennent as campaign manager, Whitefield as evangelist, and the others as helpers. One notable stop on this campaign was made at a log house at Prince Town. There was the beginning of what is now Princeton University.

On the return to Philadelphia the inhabitants showed their love for the evangelist, as usual, by a large congregation and liberal offerings. This they had contributed before, but now they went a step further and sent by boat many useful things for the orphans.

Franklin's *Pennsylvania Gazette* gives an account of his work around Philadelphia: "On Thursday last the Rev. Mr. Whitefield, left this city, and was accompanied to Chester by about one hundred and fifty horse, and preached there to about seven thousand people. On Friday he preached twice at Willings-Town to about five thousand; on Saturday at New Castle to about two thousand five hundred; and the same evening at Christiana-Bridge to about three thousand; on Sunday at Whiteclay-Creek he preached twice, resting about half an hour between the sermons, to about eight thousand, of whom about three thousand it is computed came on horseback. It rained most of the time and yet they stood in the open air." It is said by one of Mr. Whitefield's biographers that one thousand people followed him to Chester, a distance of twelve miles, and that most of them walked! This shows the esteem in which he was held by the people of Pennsylvania.

After a short stay in Philadelphia Whitefield started South, preaching as he went. His appearance in a town instantly brought a crowd together. In some places the crowd that gathered exceeded the population of the town. Tho weak in body he would preach several times a day and ride a considerable distance to the next town.

At times his course led over mountains where there was no road, and through valleys where swollen streams had to be forded.

At night he and his companions would sometimes stop at the tavern, but most of the nights were spent in private homes. In those days the wealthy farmers would set a table with cooked provisions for strangers and all who came along would be entertained. Lodging strangers was, indeed, a common and an appreciated virtue. At such a home Whitefield and his friends would sometimes stop. Sometimes the homes of rural military men would be his resting-place for the night. Everywhere, always, he preached. Whether there was only a family, a company of Negro slaves, or thousands. The sight of souls for whom Christ died still in sin was the urge that kept his message ringing out far and wide.

Many times on his journeys darkness would overtake him where there was no house of any description. In such cases a space under a tree was his

RUSSELL O. BERG

Sometimes darkness found Whitefield and his companions far from a lodging-place.

tavern and a pile of leaves his bed. On those nights
he had no soft bed high enough to push a cradle
under; no huge fireplace with tender venison in the
cook-pots was there to greet him. No warming-pan
was present to make comfortable the bed of the
traveller. When churches were refused he preached
in the open, and when he had no bed the out-of-
doors was his sleeping quarters.

Before lying down at night when he and his
companions slept out a huge fire would be built to
keep off the howling wolves. Once when about to
lie down for the night he remarked that as the wood
fire kept off the hungry wolves so "the fire of God's
love keeps the devil off."

On reaching the Potomac River where it was
six miles wide, they started to cross, and when they
were one mile out a strong wind arose. They were
finally compelled to return to shore as the wind was
too strong for them to make any headway and the
shades of night were coming on.

Whitefield reached South Carolina on New
Year's day and it so happened that a great crowd
had gathered at the house where he stopped. This
crowd was composed mostly of young people and
they had come together for the purpose of having
a dance. When they were coming no one thought
that a minister of Christ would be present! Regard-

less of the purpose for which they gathered they gave attention to the preacher as he exhorted them to purity and usefulness. He spoke to them in the evening and also in the morning.

The night following his sermon at the dance he and his companions lost the road, and seeing a light some distance away they rode near. The light came from a large fire in the open. Around the fire great crowds of slaves were dancing and carousing. The strangers stopped for a moment and feeling that the darkness was safer than the light, at this place, they turned and continued their journey.

A wearisome journey of seven hundred and fifty miles on horseback was completed when they reached Charleston. Tired from travel and turned down at the Church of England, Whitefield went to the Independent Church and preached to all that could enter the building.

The party made the rest of the journey to Savannah by water. About two days were required to row from Charleston to the port of Savannah.

While the leader of the orphans had been away his helpers and friends had been very busy at home. A portion of the five hundred acre tract of land ten miles from Savannah had been cleared and several good milk cows and a large flock of chickens had been secured. Fences had been built and also a small house in which to keep tools and supplies for the promotion of the work. Mr. Whitefield's reason for selecting a place so far from town was that the children would be near the farm where they could learn to work. It was his intention to teach them to labor so that they could earn an honest livelihood when they were old enough to leave the institution.

Whitefield's heart was bound to the work of caring for the homeless and friendless children. It was his desire to work for them "speedily as well as with all our might." The home which he was now about to build was to be called Bethesda. He says, "I call it Bethesda, that is, house of mercy; for I hope many acts of mercy will be shown there, and that many will be thereby stirred up to praise the Lord, as a God whose mercy endureth forever."

It was his practise as well as his belief to do things speedily and with all his might. He did not wait for the orphanage to be built to begin getting in the little lambs that were destitute and homeless. He rented a house where they could be kept and taught. The entry in his journal for January 29 tells of the acceptance of three German orphans. He described the poorly clothed, hungry, dirty children as "most pitiful objects" and says that if he had not received them they would never have had an opportunity to know anything about God and the truth found in his Holy Bible.

The day following the acceptance of these three orphans he went with the surveyors and the builder to survey the ground for the new home. "It is to be sixty feet long and forty feet wide; a yard and a garden before and behind. In all there will be nearly twenty commodious rooms." A house that size would be nothing out of the ordinary now, but at that period in the settlement of America it was considered almost an extravagance. Whitefield said, "I find that it will be an expensive work; but it is for the Lord Christ."

At the rented house a school was established where many who were not orphans came free, because they were unable to go to another school, and were not in reach of one to which they could be admitted.

On the twenty-first day of March, 1740, the foundation brick of the "great house" was laid. Whitefield called the workmen together and as they knelt with him in prayer he lifted his voice to God in thanksgiving for allowing such a blessed work to be started. The prayer was concluded with a benediction for those who were to have a part in the work of erecting the building. His desire for the welfare of the souls of men would not let him leave till he exhorted them always to be stedfast and abounding in the grace of the Lord Jesus.

The great preacher's sympathy for the Negro slaves was shown on the trip he made from Philadelphia. While coming along through the hills of Virginia and Carolina, and on down across the coastal plains, stopping at the homes of many slaveholders, he was in a position to observe carefully the cruel treatment of some of the slaves. His voice was raised in thundering condemnation after condemnation upon the masters who treated their servants with anything but kindness.

The kindness shown by him to those in the bondage of slavery was repaid by words of appreciation, kind looks, and very often kind deeds from those he helped. An incident showing the respect that a certain slave boy had for Whitefield was recorded by Mr. Seward, a man who was often a traveling companion of Whitefield. A certain drinking club employed the boy to wait on them, and as the boy had considerable talent as an imitator he was often called upon to mimic some character for the entertainment of those present. They asked him to mimic Whitefield, and at first the boy refused to do so. After much persuasion he stood up and said, "I speak the truth in Christ, I lie not; unless you repent you will all be damned." The words of this speech and the manner in which they were spoken caused the club to break up and never meet again.

Whitefield called himself a "gospel rover" and truly enough long and frequent journeys proved him to be one. The short visit to Savannah ended, he boarded a ship for Philadelphia. The city of brotherly love in name, and the city of brotherly love in reality on his other visits, was not so lovable on this one. Churches that were open to him then were closed now. Friends who before welcomed him now shunned him. Some were active in openly opposing him. Most of the people, however, were still kind. The opposition was caused in part by some mistakes that the evangelist had made, but perhaps most of it came from those who were unwilling to obey the truth. However, much good had been done by the previous visit. Hundreds dated a deep, personal religious experience from the time of his preaching. Many of the ministers had changed from the letter of the law as a result of Whitefield's denunciation of an unconverted ministry. One preacher acknowledged this publicly and asked the congregation to pray for him.

Even tho there was opposition from certain quarters and even tho some of the church doors were closed against him, yet thousands heard him gladly. He began preaching on Society Hill and at the first service the number of eager listeners was six thousand. Another service and there was an increase to eight thousand, and on Sunday ten thousand came to hear him. The congregation still increased until, in a few days, there were fifteen thousand present.

Franklin, who was always an attentive listener, was puzzled at the way people would continue to come when they were so plainly rebuked and condemned for their wickedness or indifference. He saw many unwilling to leave when the sermon was over, and in most all of them a change in conduct was noticeable.

While the body of Whitefield was weak, his spirits were high, and with a desire to reach the dying souls of men with a living message, he started to New York, preaching as he went. On reaching the metropolis he found people who were not only very courteous and eager to hear, but he found them also liberal. The amount of fourteen hundred and fifty-eight dollars was cheerfully given to the work of mercy at Savannah.

Returning from New York he preached as he travelled, and journeying through Philadelphia again he went to Nottingham. Here a new and strange "influence" was felt. During one of the sermons it is said that most of those present began to "melt" under the power of the preaching. Numbers began weeping and soon thousands cried out as if the judgment day had come and found them unprepared. In his account of the meeting Whitefield wrote, "Oh, what strong crying and tears were shed and poured forth after the dear Lord Jesus! Some fainted, and when they had got a little strength, would hear and faint again. Others cried out in a manner almost as if they were in the deepest agonies of death. After I had finished my last discourse I myself was so overpowered with a sense of God's love that it almost took away my life." He says further that he soon was normal again, and after taking some food he went home with a Mr. Blair who lived twenty miles away. On reaching the house they ate a meal, enjoyed the singing of several hymns, and sometime on into the hours of the morning they lay down to sleep.

At the preaching service near Mr. Blair's home the crowds were larger and the excitement greater than it had been at Nottingham. "Some were struck pale as death," says the evangelist; "others were wringing their hands, others lying on the ground, some sinking into the arms of their friends, and most of them lifting up their eyes toward heaven and crying out to God for mercy!"

Leaving hundreds rejoicing that they had found newness of life in Christ and other hundreds under

a conviction that would soon produce such a happy
state Whitefield turned his face toward Savannah
and Bethesda. He was carrying to his family gifts
collected from his friends which amounted to two
thousand three hundred and thirty dollars. The
sight of his welcome by the "little lambs" to whom
he seemed a father, mother, pastor, and teacher,
would have touched the hardest of hearts. They ran
to meet him, and with hugs and kisses wept for
joy at his coming.

The next few days in Bethesda a revival was
enjoyed as great almost as the one at Nottingham.
The orphans, the matrons, the teachers, and those
employed in clearing and building were alike overcome with religious fervor. Whitefield instructed
them, prayed with them, and all were weeping.
Many wept and prayed as they went home.

His visit home was for only a few days. Soon he
was back at Charleston, S.C., where he preached
in the Independent Church. It should be remem-
bered that Whitefield was not strong physically, and
even if he had been he could not have endured such
hardship and preached so energetically and so often
without suffering and weakness. This visit to
Charleston proved too severe for his weakened con-
stitution. He went from the church exhausted and
was unable to get back, had he not been carried on

a couch by some friends. This time when he was carried to the church to preach his last sermon on that visit, the sermon came near being his last on earth.

After the sermon he was carried back to the house where he was staying, in a pale and death-like condition. His companions in travel feared that the end was near. The host stood by weeping, and the disturbed faces of the poor slaves were seen around the window trying to get a glimpse of their friend whom they were fearful of losing. The evangelist, who never seemed to have any dread of death, was at this time eager to leave the earth and go to be with the Lord. "Surely it cannot be long," he sighed, "ere this tabernacle will be dissolved. As the hart panteth after the water brooks, so longeth my soul after the full enjoyment of thee, my God." When he felt strength returning to his body he was disappointed that the end was not yet. So many friends were praying and so much work needed to be done that he was to remain on earth a while longer and do good.

Even tho he could walk about and was able to make the trip to Savannah he was unable to stay up. He was so sure at one time that death had come that he whispered faintly, "Lord Jesus, receive my spirit." This, however, was another disappointment, for when several friends from Charleston and other places came in he began to recover. One of the friends, who was a minister, was asked to preach. If Whitefield was unable to present the gospel someone else must. But the one who was asked to preach refused and explained his reason for doing so by saying to Whitefield, "God will strengthen you." The sick went ahead to preach. As the sermon continued his strength increased, and what an effective sermon it was! Many were brought to a deep concern about the welfare of their souls. These would not have been reached if Whitefield had not preached. He was overjoyed at the result of the meeting and felt rebuked for trying to shrink the responsibility by reason of his weakness. He pleaded to the Lord, "Never let me distrust thee again."

Invitations were now coming in from prominent leaders of religion in New England. His tours had not, up to this time, reached beyond New York, but many letters of invitation had come from Dr. Coleman and Mr. Cooper of Boston. Already desiring to visit the Northeast, Whitefield readily accepted the invitation and sailed for the shores of Rhode Island. He reached Newport on a Sunday evening just in time for a preaching service. He slipped into a church, hoping to hear the sermon without being recognized. Immediately after the sermon someone guessed who he was and soon he was surrounded by ministers, distinguished laymen, and common people. He was invited to lodge in the house of a stranger and given the use of the Church of England for services.

An enthusiastic reception was given Whitefield at Boston. In fact the celebration was started several miles out of Boston, where he was met by a company of ministers and prominent gentlemen headed by the son of the Massachusetts governor. Old conservative Boston threw off its "formality" and dignity and suddenly became enthusiastic over the fiery preacher. One preacher was not glad to see him and was very free to state the fact. When he met Whitefield on the street he curtly remarked, "I am sorry to see you here." The evangelist replied, "And so is the devil!"

The governor of Massachusetts received the "gospel rover" very kindly and entered into a life-long friendship with him. He often visited Whitefield, who says concerning him, "He took me by myself and exhorted me to go on stirring up the ministers." He also urged the preacher to be bold in preaching to those in office. "Spare no one because of his position," was his good advice.

One thing in New England that made a deep impression on the evangelist was the moral purity

of the people. They were strict in observing the
old Puritan customs. Goodness with many had become a habit. Sabbath-keeping was common, in
fact it was the one outstanding religious rite of New
England. It was very pleasing to him to see the
respect there was for the day of worship.

Everywhere in England and America the problem with Whitefield was to find a place large enough
for his congregations. This was the problem in Boston. Its largest meeting-house was not large enough.
The seats would be filled with those who came
early; the aisles would be filled with those who could
not get a seat; and many would crowd around the
building as if they were expecting a miraculous
entrance to be provided.

In one such crowded place while the audience was
waiting for the preacher some little excitement
started which soon caused a panic. People were
frightened with nothing to frighten them. Some
began to scream, others began to leap out of the
gallery, and all of them made a break for the door.
Some who could not reach the door were so terrified
that they jumped out of a window. Some were
tramped upon, others bruised in some other way, and
five were taken up dead.

When it was learned that the evangelist would
preach immediately in the open the panic-stricken

people who had become more composed but greatly concerned about their souls reassembled to hear the sermon.

The Boston meetings continued for three weeks and the town was completely changed. Even tho the famous evangelist left at the close of the three weeks the revival which he was instrumental in starting continued for a year and a half. As to some of the results of the meetings it was recorded that "the very face of the town seemed to be strangely altered. Even the Negroes and boys in the streets left their usual rudeness, and taverns were found empty of all but lodgers."

The preaching against an unconverted ministry was so strong that twenty ministers in or near Boston realized that they had never been born again. They confessed their condition and asked for prayer. Thus a reformation was started in regard to the spiritual qualifications of the clergymen.

The Boston collections were as satisfactory as the spiritual results of the meeting. One of the congregations at an afternoon service gave two thousand five hundred and sixty-three dollars. On the following afternoon two thousand two hundred and eighty-four dollars were given. We are not told how much was given at the three other services during the day, but as a whole the Bostonians were very sympathetic toward the orphanage and gave liberally in contributing to its support.

The climax of the Boston meeting came at the last service when twenty thousand people were present. Many who had been converted during the meeting wept as others came crying for pardon. When Whitefield departed most of the people were in tears. The governor took his own carriage and drove the preacher to the ferry, wept, and kissed him farewell.

Invitations came from Cambridge to address the students at Harvard University. He visited Harvard several times and since he had heard reports about the lack of real Christian living among the students his preaching there was rather harsh and rebuking. However, reports came to him that "The college is entirely changed; the students are full of God; the voice of prayer and praise fills the chambers."

While in New England Whitefield made a visit to Northampton. Jonathan Edwards, the prominent minister there who started what is known as the "Great Awakening," was rather displeased with Whitefield's impulsiveness, but he appreciated the younger minister's talents and became a very close friend of his.

A tour was made through Milford, Stratford, Fairfield, Newark, and Stanford. His kind dealings

with the people at these places won him many
friends, but his harsh condemnation of unconverted
ministers brought him some enemies, especially
among those condemned. Two ministers admitted
that they had ordained some young men as ministers
without asking them if they had experienced the
work of regeneration. Another one confessed that
for years he had preached saving grace without ever
being saved by grace himself. The influence of
Whitefield's preaching to the ministers has reached
down to the present time.

One place wherein the evangelist was always welcome was Princeton, N.J. Here at the University
he was the favorite preacher. When he spoke once
in chapel and started away the students returned
to the chapel for another sermon instead of going
into their classrooms. When the University was
in need of funds, Whitefield raised money for it and
encouraged his royal friend, the Lady Huntingdon,
to support it.

On entering New York somewhat tired and
doubtful as to the results he would have, the "gospel
rover" was welcomed again by Mr. Noble. On
Friday he met a large congregation and on the evening of the same day he preached to a larger crowd.
Sunday brought a still larger crowd. When the
people crowded every part of the building the

preacher spoke with unusual earnestness, and the results were wonderful. People in all parts of the building began weeping, some weeping in the joy of a new experience and others weeping under conviction of sin.

Since Whitefield had left Philadelphia his friends there had decided to build a large structure that would accommodate a much larger congregation than any of the churches. The building was seventy feet wide and one hundred feet long. It was to be used for preaching in general and for Whitefield in particular. It was practically completed when he reached the city and he had the privilege of being the first to use it.

One interesting conversion that took place at these Philadelphia meetings was that of an atheist who had not heard Whitefield on his other visits to Philadelphia. The old man listened attentively as the preacher was discoursing on how Nicodemus came to Jesus and how Jesus said, "Ye must be born again." He reached home first and as his wife, who was a Christian, came in from the services she expressed regret that he had not heard the sermon. The former atheist said nothing. Shortly another member of the family came in and expressed the same feeling, but still the old man said nothing. But when a third member of the family came in and said,

"I wish you had heard Whitefield," he broke down with tears in his eyes and a change in his countenance and said, "I have been hearing him." The family rejoiced with him and he lived a spiritual life afterwards.

This long and fruitful "tour 'round America" ended at Savannah. On arriving there he went to Bethesda to see his family and bring his gifts. In spite of the large amounts which he collected the orphanage was still in debt. He appointed a chaplain for the orphans and put the temporal affairs of the institution under the direction of a supervisor and henceforth he was free to solicit funds and "hunt sinners" wherever he felt the call.

CHAPTER X

THE CAMBUSLANG REVIVAL

In the days of the early Methodist revivals letter-writing was a common pastime. It was enjoyed by the religious and the irreligious, but perhaps the leaders of revivals were more given to it than any other class. Whenever a fresh awakening of interest in spiritual matters would take place those who were sympathetic in distant places would write to encourage the work. For a long time Whitefield had been receiving letters from Scotland written by the Erskine brothers, Ralph and Ebenezer. He had become very affectionate with them because of their agreement on some matters of doctrine.

The Church of Scotland, like the Church of England, was none too lively as a spiritual institution, and those Christians who were zealous for holy living had withdrawn from the state church. In England they were called "Dissenters," while in Scotland a similar party was called "Seceders." The Erskines were the main figures in the reform movement in Scotland, and several times they had invited Whitefield to come and visit them. They expressed an intense longing to meet him.

He who had effected such a sweeping revival in

England and who had moved multitudes in America would be a mighty apostle to help the "Seceders," thought the Erskines. It was their purpose to get Whitefield to work with them against the state in building up the "Associate Presbytery," or "the True Presbyterian Church of Christ in Scotland," as the reform body was called by its members.

Altho the views of Whitefield and the Erskines on points of doctrine were practically the same, there was no harmony as to a system of church government. The Erskines believed a particular form of government was Biblical and rejected all others. Whitefield, with his sympathetic heart and broad views, was more catholic. He was determined to preach Christ in any place wherever he was invited. He even said if he was invited by a Mohammedan he would accept the invitation and condemn Mohammed by declaring salvation through Christ alone. So he came to Scotland to preach the simple gospel as it is in Christ and not to join with a faction.

He landed at Leith in July, 1741, and as soon as he landed the two rival factions tried to win him to their position. The state church wanted him and the Seceders wanted him. He was invited by the state church to preach in Edinburgh on the same day that he landed. The invitation was not accepted, but a service was announced for the evening.

Then he went directly to Dunfernline to see the Erskines.

At Dunfernline he preached to the congregation of Ralph Erskine's and after the sermon he said that they wanted to talk to him and "set him right about church government." He had no time to talk for he had to hurry back to Edinburgh and preach as he had agreed to do. He agreed however, to meet the Associate Presbytery in a few days in Mr. Ralph's house.

He was back to meet them in due time. The presbytery consisted of Ralph and Ebenezer Erskine and five others who were ministers or prominent laymen. Most of them thought that Whitefield would join them immediately, but some of the more thoughtful only hoped to pave the way for his union with them later. Whitefield could not accept the presbyterian form of government, but kept his determination to go where he was called.

Scotland was in a great commotion about religion, and perhaps as much so about Whitefield. He started preaching in Edinburgh. The results were gratifying. The most wicked and wayward boys in the city were converted. Prayer-meetings were established and carried on with frequency and power. It was on this visit that admirers of the great preacher tried to give him a personal contribution, but he declined it saying, "I make no purse; what I have I give away." He was earnest in getting money for the orphans, but he had no time for personal material ambitions.

Preaching excursions were made from Edinburgh and numbers of towns welcomed him and enjoyed the fruits of his labor. One of the preaching excursions carried him to Aberdeen. At this place he preached for Mr. Ogilive, who had an associate pastor with an uncharitable disposition. At the next service the associate had charge and in the midst of his prayer he entreated the Lord to forgive the dishonor that had been put upon him by Mr. Whitefield's being allowed to preach in the pulpit. Whitefield took the gibe good-naturedly and with the invitation of Mr. Ogilive was, within thirty minutes, preaching in the pulpit again.

The work of the evangelist in Scotland was abruptly cut off by his going to Wales to get married. The marriage occurred in Abergavenny, Wales, on November 14, 1741. He was twenty-six years old. Mrs. James, a widow, who became his wife, was thirty-six. Little is known of the courtship, but if one should judge by some of Whitefield's love letters that have been published he would quickly decide that he was a greater preacher than he was a love-maker. His wife had been a good Christian for a number of years. Mr. Wesley commended her as "a woman of candor and humanity."

After spending the winter in London Whitefield sailed with his wife for Scotland to continue his work there. Being very fatigued from constant preaching and the weight of opposition, he spent most of the voyage in secret prayer. It was June, 1742, when he landed at Leith and many of his friends were so glad to see him that they walked and followed his coach from Leith to Edinburgh, a distance of almost two miles.

"The Associate Presbytery" was not glad to see him. Even his good friends, the Erskines, were not friendly with him. Adam Gid, one of the Associate Presbytery, published and circulated a fifty-page sermon against Whitefield. He endeavored to show that Whitefield was not a minister of Jesus Christ, that he was not orderly in his practise, and that some of the doctrines he preached were diabolical. Therefore it was Gid's duty to "warn" the people to stay away from preaching that was done on any day except Sunday, and to stay away from Whitefield even on Sunday! He declared further in the "warning" that it was a duty of the people to God, to the church, to themselves, and to their fellowmen to stay away from Whitefield.

The warning of Gid was merely amusing to

many; it served as good advertising to others; and heedless of it the multitudes came pouring in to hear a preacher who had a message and who stood above strife and factionalism. Twice a day people flocked to the Hospital Park in Edinburgh. If he was in demand in Edinburgh he was doubly so in Cambuslang. This suburb of Glasgow was then a village of nine hundred people.

Rev. William McCollough, the good pastor at Cambuslang, had read about the revival in England and America, and as he read the news he would pass it on to the members of his congregation. They desired to have such a work among themselves and prayed for it. The result was that a new interest was awakened in religion to such an extent that the church would not accommodate the people. With a desire to save more people the good pastor moved the services to a small valley near the church. The congregation assembled in the valley, which formed a natural amphitheater, and heard the pastor stress the need of regeneration.

When Whitefield reached Cambuslang he found a revival already in progress. Some who were there had heard him preach, others had read his sermons, and nearly all had heard of him and were overjoyed to see him. McCollough was preaching daily, and one day so many penitents came for instruction that he was busy most of the night. Three hundred had been awakened, and two hundred of them had been genuinely converted.

Many people had quit drinking and cursing and had become absorbed in making restitution for what had been taken by fraud, having family prayer, and reading their Bibles. All classes were reached and inspired with religious fervor.

On Tuesday, at noon, Whitefield preached his first sermon. A second one came at six, and again at nine he began to preach. At eleven there was a commotion. Conviction seized the sinners. Others wept from feeling the presence of God. Thousands wept and sometimes their wails would drown the voice of the preacher. When Whitefield finished, the pastor began and preached till one o'clock in the morning. Multitudes then would not go home. They walked the fields singing and praying.

When Saturday came more than twenty thousand people were present. The Lord's Supper was to be observed on Sunday. Two tents were erected for the communion service, and when Whitefield started to break the bread so many people thronged around the tables that he was constrained to preach to them. He started what proved to be an all-day preaching service. There was not a time during the whole day but that someone was preaching. At the Sunday

evening service Whitefield preached for an hour
and a half. Rain fell during most of the services,
but twenty thousand were so interested that they
hardly moved. The Monday following the sacrament Sunday was almost as exciting as the Sunday
itself.

Whitefield suddenly became ill and almost de-
spaired of life. In writing of it he said, "Last night
some of my friends thought I was going off. But
how did Jesus fill my heart! Today I am, as they
call it, much better. In less than a month we are to
have another sacrament at Cambuslang—a thing not
practised before in Scotland. I entreat all to pray
in an especial manner for a blessing at that time."

This second sacrament was a greater celebration
than the first. Between thirty and forty thousand
people were present, three thousand of whom were
able to get to the table to partake of the bread and
wine in commemoration of the death of our Lord as
a ransom for many.

Chapter XI

WHITEFIELD'S SOUL TRAP

Moorsfield, tho dedicated to the frivolities of the world, became one of the greatest soul-saving stations in England. Whitefield preached there from a wrestler's stage, from his field pulpit, and the time came when it occurred to him that a permanent place in that field was needed. In order that regular attendants might be cared for, and so that the services could be held under protection from rain, sunshine, and cold, the building was started. It was finished in about two months and called "the Tabernacle." One writer called it a "large wooden shed." Whitefield was a pioneer in the building of wooden tabernacles for evangelistic meetings.

Meetings were started in the new Tabernacle in 1741. The congregations grew rapidly from the first, and during the whole winter of 1741-1742 services were held in the Tabernacle, with fruitful results. However, Whitefield's preaching was not confined to the Tabernacle during this stay in London. He would preach in other parts of Moorsfield and London, and after preaching he would invite the hearers to the permanent Tabernacle.

At these various places he was not always a welcome guest by the crowds. For, if his preaching had stopped the common amusements of Philadelphia it was sure to hinder these more vile practises of a more sensual people. Once he wrote, "I was honored with having a few stones, rotten eggs, and pieces of dead cat thrown at me, whilst engaged in calling them from their favorite but lying vanities."

From the place where the above "honor" was given him he went to the Tabernacle with the people following. Concerning this experience he wrote, "We then returned to the Tabernacle, with my pockets full of notes from persons brought under concern, and read them amid the praises and spiritual acclamations of thousands, who joined with the holy angels in rejoicing that so many sinners, in such an unexpected, unlikely place and manner were snatched from the very jaws of the devil. This was the beginning of the Tabernacle Society. Three hundred and fifty awakened souls were received in one day, and I believe the number of notes exceeded a thousand."

The crowds that came to the Tabernacle at first were a low, illiterate class of people such as were found in the mines and in Moorsfield revels. They were truly, as Whitefield expressed it, snatched "out of the very jaws of the devil." One of those converted was a man who had given his wife and three dollars and thirty-five cents for a neighbor's wife. Many of the others were as low.

It must not be thought, however, that all who came to the wooden Tabernacle were low or even common people. Many of the English nobility came to hear the gospel. The more religious among them and the most frequent attendants were the Earl and Countess of Huntingdon. Other distinguished people who came were the Ladies Hastings, the Duke of Cumberland, the Prince of Wales, Lord Hervey, the Duke of Bolton, Lord Beaucler, and Lord Lonsdale. Like Paul, Whitefield was a chosen vessel to bear the name of the Lord before kings.

When the rich and the aristocrats came to hear Whitefield they heard the same clear gospel message that was preached to anyone else. The audience might change, but the gospel, never.

In 1748 Whitefield was invited to preach in the drawing-room of the Countess of Huntingdon. At this meeting many of the nobility heard the great evangelist. The Earl of Chesterfield said to him at one of these services, "I will not tell you what I shall tell others, how I approve of you."

The Lady Huntingdon became one of Whitefield's converts and labored with him for the salvation of souls till his death. She appointed him as

one of her chaplains and gave considerable money
for the support of his work.

Whitefield desired to have a permanent meeting-
place in the fashionable West End of London,
where he would be able to reach more of the society
folks and the nobility. This hope of another meeting
place was realized in 1756 when the Tottenham
Court Chapel was completed. It was a large building, dignified in appearance, with a dome one
hundred and fourteen feet high. It was an aristo-
cratic center of religious activity. Shortly after it
was opened Whitefield wrote, "God is doing won-
ders in the new chapel. A neighboring doctor had
baptized the place, calling it 'Whitefield's Soul
Trap.' I pray that it may be a soul-trap indeed, to
many wandering sinners."

The first building stood as a soul-saving station
for one hundred and thirty-three years. Then the
original building was torn down and replaced by a
more accommodating and up-to-date building. This
spot is still hallowed by its religious influences, and
today, after nearly two centuries of constant use,
it is still what Whitefield prayed that it would be—
a "soul trap."

While the work was prospering in London much
of Whitefield's time was spent in what he called
"cross plowing the land." He made preaching tours

into Wales, Ireland, Scotland, and also on the Continent. Spain was included on one of his excursions. He preached as he went and as he came. Multitudes listened wherever he went. He was constantly about the business of the King, and the King was with him.

CHAPTER XII

THE PROPHET'S POWER

In order to get an understanding of the preacher let us first look at Whitefield, the man. In body he was well proportioned, slender (except in later life), and remarkably graceful in manners. His countenance was fair, and his eyes were a dark blue.

Everything about his person was in order. His hat, his gloves, and other articles of clothing were not only neat and clean, but they were scrupulously kept in place while not in use. He always wore the bands, gown, and cassock common to clergymen in his day, and his appearance and manly bearing were such as always commanded respect and attention.

A weak brother who stumbled at Whitefield's neatness and order in dress made a complaint against the preacher. The complainer received the following statements in a letter: "I could not but smile to find you wink at the decency of my dress. Alas! my brother, I have known long since what it is to be in that state you are, in my opinion, about to enter into. I myself once thought that Christianity required me to go nasty. I neglected myself as much as you would have me for a twelve-month; but when God gave me the spirit of adoption, I then dressed decently, as you call it, out of principle, and I am more and more convinced that the Lord would have me act in this respect as I do."

Whitefield was as particular and exact in his other habits as he was about his clothes. It was his custom to go to bed at ten o'clock and rise at four each morning. Matters that changed his schedule for the day must be of some importance. He would interrupt a conversation at ten in the evening and say, "It is time for all good folks to be at home." It was his desire to have the table properly spread at meal time regardless of the amount or kind of food that was served. And he was displeased with late meals. Time was always valuable to him, and sometimes when people called on him for some trivial cause he would instruct them to "come back at five o'clock in the morning." Even tho he was punctual and exacting Wesley says that he was "susceptible to the most generous and most tender friendships." He despised heated arguments and was penitent when found in error. His friends were asked to "entreat God to give me humility, so shall success not be my ruin."

In his family relations Whitefield was dutiful and loving. He loved privacy and spent as much time at home as he could and at the same time do the work of an evangelist.

As a writer he never produced anything worthy of special notice. A number of volumes of sermons and other works from his pen were published. Even tho they were widely read at home and abroad and accomplished great good, yet the preacher's power was not revealed in his written works.

As a preacher Whitefield stood head and shoulders above those of his day. He had a live message in a period of religious deadness. He was verily a prophet of the Lord—a voice crying in the wilderness. The melody of his voice always captivated his hearers, and as to volume he could speak to a mere handful of people in a private home and adapt his voice to the occasion, and go right out in the open and speak so as to be heard by thousands. David Gerrick, the noted actor, said, "I would give five hundred dollars if I could only say 'Oh' like Mr. Whitefield." Gerrick also said that Whitefield could make an audience weep or tremble by his varied utterance of the word "Mesopotamia."

A well-known shipbuilder was persuaded to hear Whitefield and throughout the sermon he listened eagerly. When asked what he thought of Whitefield he exclaimed, "Think! I never heard such a man in my life. I tell you, sir, every Sunday when

I go to church I can build a ship from stem to stern under the sermon; but were it to save my soul, under Mr. Whitefield I could not lay a single plank."

The earnestness of the preacher was always manifest. He could hardly picture a lost soul without weeping. Neither could he describe the love and sufferings of Christ without a flood of joy coming over his soul and tears coming into his eyes. His passion for the souls of men was one of the secrets of his success. His power was not altogether in the control of his voice, even tho that was perfect, nor was it in the particularity of his enunciation, nor the natural grace of his movement. These were helpful in making him useful, but back of them was a vision of men lost in sin and an all-consuming conviction that the gospel was "the power of God unto salvation to all that believe." He preached as if each sermon were going to be the last.

As remarkable as his power to preach a sermon was his ability to keep on preaching sermon after sermon, year after year. Once in the middle of winter he preached nineteen times in four days. In Edinburgh he preached sixteen times in three days. At another time he preached seven times in one day, at the close of which he wrote, "They that wait on the Lord shall renew their strength; they shall mount up on wings like eagles."

He paid the price of being a great preacher. From Edinburgh he wrote to a friend, "By preaching always twice, once thrice, and once four times in a day, I am quite weakened, but I hope to recruit again. I am burning with a fever, and have a violent cold, but Christ's presence makes me smile at pain; and the fire of his love burns up all fevers." Often at the close of a sermon he would have painful vomitings, loss of appetite, and untold suffering. He said, "I know what nervous disorders are." But he continued, "Blessed be God that they were contracted in his service!"

David Hume, the great scientist and philosopher, who was not very friendly with evangelical preachers, declared that he would go twenty miles to hear Whitefield. Hume took great pleasure in repeating a few select sayings from Whitefield's sermon, then he would tell his friends, "This address surpassed anything I ever saw or heard in any other preacher."

Lord Bolingbroke said, "Mr. Whitefield is the most extraordinary man in our times. He has the most commanding eloquence I ever heard in any person."

When Whitefield was compelled by weakness to preach only once a day on week days and three times on Sundays he said that he was on "short allowance." He was distressed at being able to preach so little. It was a common thing for him to spend forty hours a week in actual preaching. Many times the number of hours was sixty.

Charles Haddon Spurgeon, after reading a volume containing seventy-five of Whitefield's sermons, said, "In these sermons one perceives the coals of Jupiter and hot thunderbolts, which mark him out to be a true Boanerges (son of thunder)."

He was a preacher, says Benjamin Franklin, "who could at any time and anywhere, collect in the open air, an audience of many thousands, without offering a single heretical novelty."

This evangelist was truly an instrument in the hands of God to turn multitudes "from darkness to light, and from the power of Satan unto God."

Chapter XIII

RESULTS OF THE STRENUOUS LIFE

The life of Whitefield is an excellent example of what the late Theodore Roosevelt called "the strenuous life." Whitefield read; he wrote letters; he wrote books; he helped orphans; he preached to prisoners, and he preached to kings! "No nestling" was one of his mottoes. There is written in the book of the deeds of men the fact that in a career of thirty-four years he preached eighteen thousand sermons.

First among the results of such a wonderful life we shall mention those who were converted by his preaching. In all parts of Great Britain, England, Ireland, Scotland, and Wales, his converts were numerous. In America from Boston to Savannah his converts could be counted by the hundreds. It is also a notable fact that many of his converts were from the class of people who seldom go to church.

It must not be thought, however, that most of his followers were of a low class of people. It is true that many of the riff-raff were changed to an upright life by his preaching, but gentlemen of brilliant intellect and refined tastes followed him by the scores. Thomas Olivers, who wrote the hymn, "The

God of Abraham, Praise," was a convert of White-field's. So was Robert Robinson, the famous Cambridge minister who wrote, "Come Thou Fount of Every Blessing," and John Faucett, who is the author of "Blest Be the Tie That Binds."

In and around Boston there were at one time twenty preachers who were spiritual children of Whitefield. Some of them became almost as useful in the ministry as was their spiritual father.

The converts of Whitefield were not all in the countries in which he preached. In 1900 a man in Australia who was converted by reading White-field's sermons sent a liberal offering to London to aid in the erection of a new building on the grounds where Tottingham Court Chapel was first built.

Another great accomplishment of the evangelist's labors was the impetus he gave to works of charity. He was moved with compassion for those in distress and he was capable of stirring up benevolence in others. His noble work for prisoners, slaves, homeless, and other unfortunate people awakened a new and keen interest in philanthropy. Many benevolent and missionary societies were formed as a direct or an indirect result of his influence. A great missionary movement followed the eighteenth century revival, and no one can tell to what extent Whitefield's work influenced it.

One writer calls Whitefield the originator of the modern evangelical revival. Indeed he was a pioneer in this field of Christian work. He traveled from place to place, and his ability to draw large congregations in churches, in tabernacles, and in fields was marvelous. His bold and incessant fighting against sin accustomed the religious world to the idea of aggressiveness.

His life and practise was a rebuke to sectarianism. A few modern writers seem to depreciate his life because he did not found another denomination. He would not cause divisions among Christians. He was a world evangelist and he recognized Christians as brethren wherever he met them.

He was always interested in proper education and he did a great service to the American people through his efforts for Princeton and Dartmouth colleges. Considerable sums of money were brought from England by him for both of these institutions. Also he had planned to open a school in Pennsylvania for Negroes whom he intended to buy and set free. After some of the buildings were erected the plan failed because of the death of Mr. Seward, who was to furnish a large share of the funds and manage the details.

Whitefield's clear and earnest preaching changed the whole fabric of the preaching of his day. He drew a line between a converted and an unconverted ministry in bold and striking terms. He appealed for a God-called and a God-sent ministry and to a great extent such a ministry followed his labors.

As stated he did not found a denomination, but he did much to mould the spiritual life of several. The Church of England and the Dissenters as well, were revived by his work. The Presbyterian Church in America bears the marks of his ministry. Many local congregations were established by his work. He connected the religious influences of the "Holy Club" of England with the "Great Awakening" in America.

It was mostly through his influence that the "caste" system of seating and dealing with college students at Harvard and Yale was abolished.

Thus he went about doing good from the time he entered the ministry in 1735 till his death in 1770. Of these thirty-four strenuous years two were spent at sea (he crossed the Atlantic thirteen times), nine were spent in America, and about twenty-three in Great Britain.

For over a quarter of a century he was a mighty "voice," a herald of glad tidings of peace. His burning passion was to win souls for whom Christ died, and in order to do that he averaged ten sermons a week for a period of thirty-four years!

The spirit of this soldier of the cross will, indeed, shine like the stars, for it is known throughout the world that he turned many to righteousness.

Chapter XIV

DYING IN BATTLE

"I am determined to die fighting." These words of the famous evangelist show us of what metal he was. At fifty he was, according to Wesley, "an old, old, man." Afflicted in body, he sailed for America on September 4, 1769, on his thirteenth voyage. After a long and tempestuous voyage he landed at Georgia in December. Here he spent the winter months at Bethesda among those children whom he called his prizes. These whom he had supported and prayed for were now a blessing to him in ministering to his comfort in his closing days.

The spring of 1770 arrived and with it a new vigor came to the evangelist. He started on a preaching tour through the North. This tour proved a great blessing to him. Old friendships were renewed. Many old enemies had become warm friends. Invitations to preach crowded in upon him as never before. Everywhere he was welcomed, and he preached to immense crowds with power.

Everywhere he went there was a crowd, but now he was not always physically able to meet it. The inward man was renewed day by day while the body was weakened. "Oh, for a warm heart!" he would

He spent the winter among the children at Bethesda.

exclaim, and his heart was still aflame for souls. But the body had grown corpulent and other afflictions came on.

He started for Newburyport, Mass., on Friday, September 28, expecting to preach there the following Sunday. On the way he stopped to preach at Exeter. Before the sermon at Exeter, which proved to be his last one, someone said to him, "You are more fit to go to bed than to preach." He agreed that the statement was true and then prayed, "Lord Jesus, I am weary *in* thy work, but not *of* thy work. If I have not yet finished my course, let me go and speak for thee once more in the fields, seal thy truth, and come home and die."

He mounted a large hogshead to address the multitudes. With a pale face and an erect body he stood speechless. Finally, with effort he said, "I wait for the gracious assistance of God, for he will, I am certain, assist me once more to speak in his name." In the course of the sermon he said, "I go to a rest prepared; my sun has arisen, and by and by from heaven it will give light to many; now it is about to set—no, it is to rise to the zenith of immortal glory. I have outlived many on earth, but they cannot outlive me in heaven. My body fails but my spirit expands. How willingly I would live forever to preach Christ! But I die to be with him!"

For two hours he preached with his face "shining like the unclouded sun." After the sermon he went directly to Newburyport to the home of his old friend and fellow-minister, Mr. Parsons. At supper he ate very little and shortly after he excused himself and started to bed. As he ascended the stairs the hall and yard were crowded with eager faces who desired to hear him speak. He turned to face them and began an exhortation. Words flowed freely. His eyes were wet with tears as he spoke to them until the candle which he held in his hand had burned up and gone out.

When he reached the bedroom he read some in his Bible, committed himself to God, and lay down. In the early morning he awoke suffering. Being unable to rise and pray as he often did at night he sat up in bed and prayed that more souls might be brought to Christ. He asked God to guide him, to bless the orphans, to bless the worshipers at the chapels, and to bless his friends.

At the close of the prayer he lay down again but soon he called for help. "My asthma—my asthma is coming on." Panting for breath he struggled toward an open window and said to his attendant, "I am dying! I am dying!"

Thus at six o'clock on Sunday morning, September 30, 1770, George Whitefield rested from his labors. His death brought to a close one of the most remarkable careers that ever blessed and benefitted the church and mankind generally. His death was in many respects as he had hoped it would be. He was not only ready to die but eager to meet his Lord, for he often had exclaimed, "Fly, fly, O time! Welcome, welcome, long-looked for eternity!"

CHAPTER XV

EXTRACTS FROM WHITEFIELD'S SERMON
ON "THE METHOD OF GRACE"

(This great sermon was preached in the High-Church yard of Glasgow, Scotland, on Sunday morning, September 13, 1741.)

"They have healed also the hurt of the daughter of my people slightly, saying, peace, peace; when there is no peace."—Jer. 6:14

The prophet gives a thundering message, that they might be terrified and have some convictions and inclinations to repent; but it seems that the false prophets, the false priests, went about stifling people's convictions, and when they were hurt or a little terrified, they were for daubing over the wound, telling them that Jeremiah was but an enthusiastic preacher, that there could be no such thing as war among them, and saying to people, Peace, peace, be still, when the prophet told them there was no peace. The words, then, refer primarily unto outward things but I verily believe have also a further reference to the soul, and are to be referred to those false teachers, who when people were under conviction of sin, when people were beginning to look towards heaven, were for stifling

123

their convictions and telling them they were good
enough before. And, indeed, people generally love
to have it so; our hearts are exceedingly deceitful,
and desperately wicked; none but the eternal God
knows how *treacherous* they are.

We are all desirous of peace; peace is an unspeakable blessing; how can we live without peace? And,
therefore, people from time to time must be taught
how far they must go, and what must be wrought
in them, before they can speak peace to their hearts.
This is what I design at present, that I may deliver
my soul, that I may be free from the blood of all
those to whom I preach—that I may not fail to
declare the whole counsel of God. I shall, from the
words of the text, endeavor to show you what you
must undergo, and what must be wrought in you
before you can speak peace to your *hearts.*

First, then, before you can speak peace to your
hearts, you must be made to see, made to feel, made
to weep over, made to bewail, your actual transgressions against the law of God. According to the
covenant of works, "The soul that sinneth; it shall
die"; cursed is that man, be he what he may, be
he who he may, that continueth not in all things
that are written in the book of the law to do them.
We are not only to do some things, but we are to
do all things, and we are to continue so to do; so

that the least deviation from the moral law, according to the covenant of works, whether in thought, word, or deed, deserves eternal death at the hand of God. And if one evil thought, if one evil word, if one evil action, deserves eternal damnation, how many hells, my friends, do every one of us deserve, whose whole lives have been one continued rebellion against God! Before ever, therefore, you can speak peace to your hearts, you must be brought to see, brought to believe, what a dreadful thing it is to depart from the living God. And now, my dear friends, examine your hearts, for I hope you came hither with a design to have your souls made better. Give me leave to ask you, in the presence of God, whether you know the time, and if you do not know exactly the time do you know there was a time, when God wrote bitter things against you, when the arrows of the the Almighty were within you? Was ever the remembrance of your sins grievous to you? Was the burden of your sins intolerable to your thoughts? Did you ever see that God's wrath might justly fall upon you, on account of your actual transgressions against God? Were you ever in all your life sorry for your sins? Could you ever say, My sins are gone over my head as a burden too heavy for me to bear? Did you ever experience any such thing as this? Did ever any such thing as this pass between God and

your soul? If not, for Jesus Christ's sake, do not
call yourselves Christians; you may speak peace to
your hearts, but there is no peace. May the Lord
awaken you, may the Lord convert you, may the
Lord give you peace, if it be his will, before you
go home!

Further: before you can speak peace to your
hearts, you must not only be troubled for the sins
of your life, the sins of your nature, but likewise for
the sins of your best duties and performances. When
a poor soul is somewhat awakened by the terrors of
the Lord, then the poor creature, being born under
the covenant of works, flies directly to a covenant
of works again. And as Adam and Eve hid themselves among the trees of the garden, and sewed fig
leaves together to cover their nakedness, so the poor
sinner, when awakened, flies to his duties and to
his performances to hide himself from God, and
goes to patch up a righteousness of his own. Says
he, I will be mighty good now—I will reform—I
will do all I can; and then certainly Jesus Christ
will have mercy on me. But before you can speak
peace to your heart, you must be brought to see that
God may damn you for the best prayer you every
put up; you must be brought to see that all your
duties—all your righteousness—as the prophet ele-
gantly expresses it—put them all together, are so

far from recommending you to God, are so far from being any motive and inducement to God to have mercy on your poor soul, that he will see them to be filthy rags, a menstruous cloth—that God hates them, and cannot away with them, if you bring them to him in order to recommend you to his favor. My dear friends, what is there in our performances to recommend us unto God?

"Come," says Jesus, "unto me, all ye that are weary and heavy laden, and I will give you rest." This speaks encouragement to all that are weary and heavy laden; but the promise of rest is made to them only upon their coming and believing, and taking him to be their God and their all. Before we can ever have peace with God, we must be justified by faith through our Lord Jesus Christ, we must be enabled to apply Christ to our hearts, we must have Christ brought home to our souls, so as his righteousness may be made our righteousness, so as his merits may be imputed to our souls. My dear friends, were you ever married to Jesus Christ? Did Jesus Christ ever give himself to you? Did you ever close with Christ by a lively faith, so as to feel Christ in your hearts, so as to hear him speaking peace to your souls? Did peace ever flow in upon your hearts like a river? Did you ever feel that peace that Christ spoke to his disciples? I pray God he may come and speak peace to you. These things you must experience. I am not talking of the invisible realities of another world, of inward religion, of the work of God upon a poor sinner's heart. I am now talking of a matter of great importance, my dear hearers; you are all concerned in it, your souls are concerned in it, your eternal salvation is concerned in it. You may be all at peace, but perhaps the devil has lulled you asleep into a carnal lethargy and security, and will endeavor to keep you there, till he gets you to hell, and there you will be awakened; but it will be dreadful to be awakened and find yourselves so fearfully mistaken, when the great gulf is fixed, when you will be calling to all eternity for a drop of water to cool your tongue, and shall not obtain it.

There is a great multitude of souls here; how shortly must you all die, and go to judgment! Even before night, or tomorrow's night, some of you may be laid out for this kirk-yard. And how will you do if you be not at peace with God—if the Lord Jesus Christ has not spoken peace to your heart? If God speak not peace to you here, you will be damned forever. I must not flatter you, my dear friends, I will deal sincerely with your souls. Some of you may think I carry things too far. But, indeed, when you come to judgment, you will find what I say is true.

THE END